Man Enough? Measuring Masculine Norms to Promote Women's Empowerment

OECD **dev**

DEVELOPMENT CENTRE

This work is published under the responsibility of the Secretary-General of the OECD. The opinions expressed and arguments employed herein do not necessarily reflect the official views of the member countries of the OECD or its Development Centre.

This document, as well as any data and map included herein, are without prejudice to the status of or sovereignty over any territory, to the delimitation of international frontiers and boundaries and to the name of any territory, city or area.

The statistical data for Israel are supplied by and under the responsibility of the relevant Israeli authorities. The use of such data by the OECD is without prejudice to the status of the Golan Heights, East Jerusalem and Israeli settlements in the West Bank under the terms of international law.

Note by Turkey
The information in this document with reference to "Cyprus" relates to the southern part of the Island. There is no single authority representing both Turkish and Greek Cypriot people on the Island. Turkey recognises the Turkish Republic of Northern Cyprus (TRNC). Until a lasting and equitable solution is found within the context of the United Nations, Turkey shall preserve its position concerning the "Cyprus issue".

Note by all the European Union Member States of the OECD and the European Union
The Republic of Cyprus is recognised by all members of the United Nations with the exception of Turkey. The information in this document relates to the area under the effective control of the Government of the Republic of Cyprus.

Please cite this publication as:
OECD (2021), *Man Enough? Measuring Masculine Norms to Promote Women's Empowerment*, Social Institutions and Gender Index, OECD Publishing, Paris, *https://doi.org/10.1787/6ffd1936-en*.

ISBN 978-92-64-69998-4 (print)
ISBN 978-92-64-70705-4 (pdf)

Social Institutions and Gender Index
ISSN 2663-4716 (print)
ISSN 2663-4724 (online)

Preface

For the last decade, the OECD Development Centre's Social Institutions and Gender Index (SIGI) has supported countries in understanding the often invisible barriers to women and girls' empowerment by measuring the levels of discrimination in social institutions. While the gender equality discourse has predominantly focused on discrimination against women and girls, it is increasingly clear that men and boys need to be engaged in achieving gender equality. The issue thus becomes: how can men and boys be included in advancing important goals such as promoting women's participation in the labour market, equally redistributing domestic and care work among household members, ensuring women's political representation and eradicating violence against women? This in turn requires challenging unequal gender power dynamics which are built on codified relations between men and women and on what it means to "be a 'real' man". In other words, we need to reassess and rethink the ways in which masculinities can be supportive of greater equality, in the context of the Agenda 2030 on sustainable development

When the OECD Development Centre convened a group of experts in February 2020 to discuss the inclusion of masculinities in the Social Institutions and Gender Index (SIGI) framework, it became clear that a major barrier to a more systemic understanding of, and solutions to, restrictive masculinities, was a lack of available and comparable data. This publication responds to the urgent need to fill this gap. First, it identifies ten norms of restrictive masculinities that need to urgently be addressed. Second, it proposes a series of indicators designed to measure these norms using a "SIGI lens" by analysing legal frameworks, attitudes and associated practices.

By measuring change over time, these indicators can provide evidence on the effectiveness of policies and programmes aimed at transforming restrictive masculinities into gender-equitable ones. Moreover, this analysis can reshape the gender equality discourse which is often viewed as a zero-sum effort, where women benefit at the expense of men. Taking a serious look at masculinities reveals that the same masculine norms harming women and girls and their empowerment, are also detrimental to the well-being of men and boys, as well as the inclusion of LGBTI people. In short, systematically analysing masculinities can accelerate gender research and demonstrate that achieving gender equality benefits all people.

Mario Pezzini
Director, OECD Development Centre
Special Advisor to the OECD Secretary-General on Development

Foreword

Since 2009, the OECD Development Centre has used the Social Institutions and Gender Index (SIGI) to shed light on the often invisible barriers to women's and girls' empowerment in developing and developed countries. One of the SIGI's unique aspects is its focus on measuring and analysing the social norms that promote discriminatory practices. This publication enriches this work in its focus on masculinities – social constructions of what it means to "be a 'real' man" – which can either hinder or promote women's empowerment and gender equality. Despite a growing recognition that masculine norms need to be addressed, efforts to do so are hindered by a lack of comparable data.

Man Enough? Measuring Masculine Norms to Promote Women's Empowerment identifies and describes the ten norms of restrictive masculinities that are most obstructive to women's empowerment and gender equality in the economic, political and private spheres. It provides a roadmap for future efforts to measure changing masculinities by suggesting indicators – both "ideal" indicators and available proxies – for all ten norms of restrictive masculinities defined in this report. It makes the case that addressing restrictive masculinities is a key part of promoting women's empowerment and that collecting the right data to measure norms of masculinities is not only possible but indispensable to achieve the 2030 Agenda on Sustainable Development.

Acknowledgements

Man Enough? Measuring Masculine Norms to Promote Women's Empowerment was prepared by the OECD Development Centre under the supervision of Mario Pezzini, Director of the OECD Development Centre and Special Advisor to the OECD Secretary-General on Development, and Bathylle Missika, Head of the Networks, Partnerships and Gender Division. Led by Hyeshin Park and Gaëlle Ferrant, the report was drafted by Gaëlle Ferrant, Gabrielle Naumann-Woleske and Sarah Stummbillig. The production of the report was co-ordinated by Gabrielle Naumann-Woleske, Policy Analyst with the Gender Programme. The report was edited by Brenda O'Hanlon. Many thanks go to the OECD Development Centre's Publication and Communications team, Henri-Bernard Solignac-Lecomte, Aida Buendia, Delphine Grandrieux, Elizabeth Nash, Laura Parry-Davies and Mélodie Descours.

The report benefited from insights from several OECD colleagues, including Pierre de Boisséson, Giacomo Gattorno, Alejandra Meneses, Hyeshin Park and Bathylle Missika, as well as Charlotte Goemans, Jenny Hedman, Elizabeth Holbourne, Seve Loudon, Cecilia Mezzanotte and Marie-Anne Valfort. We would also like to highlight the support of Grace Dunphy and Sonja Marki.

The OECD Development Centre would also like to extend its gratitude to the experts who joined the Expert Group Meeting in February 2020 focused on "Defining and examining masculinities through the Social Institutions and Gender Index (SIGI) Framework". The report has benefited greatly from the specific inputs of Gary Barker, Marlon Bascombe, Caroline de Cremoux, Kate Doyle, Fabrice Ferrier, Maria Lohan, Emilija Milenković, Alexander Munive, Manika Rana, Raikamal Roy, Ravi Verma and Kislay Yadav.

The OECD Development Centre is particularly grateful to the Austrian Development Agency (ADA) for its financial support and collaboration in carrying out this research within the project, "From data to policy action: addressing social institutions governing women's and men's behaviour to enhance gender equality".

Table of contents

FIGURES

TABLES

Follow OECD Publications on:

http://twitter.com/OECD_Pubs

http://www.facebook.com/OECDPublications

http://www.linkedin.com/groups/OECD-Publications-4645871

http://www.youtube.com/oecdilibrary

http://www.oecd.org/oecddirect/

This book has...

StatLinks

A service that delivers Excel® files from the printed page!

Look for the *StatLinks* at the bottom of the tables or graphs in this book. To download the matching Excel® spreadsheet, just type the link into your Internet browser, starting with the *https://doi.org* prefix, or click on the link from the e-book edition.

Abbreviations and acronyms

BPfA	Beijing Declaration and Platform for Action
CEDAW	Convention on the Elimination of All Forms of Discrimination against Women
CEO	chief executive officer
DHS	Demographic and Health Surveys
EIGE	European Institute for Gender Equality
EU	European Union
HIV	human immunodeficiency virus
ICRW	International Center for Research on Women
ICT	information and communication technology
ILO	International Labour Organization
IMAGES	International Men and Gender Equality Survey
IPU	Inter-Parliamentary Union
ISCO	International Standard Classification of Occupations
LGBTI	lesbian, gay, bisexual, transgender and intersex
MENA	Middle East and North Africa
MSCI	Morgan Stanley Capital International
NGO	non-governmental organisation
OECD	Organisation for Economic Co-operation and Development
PISA	Programme for International Student Assessment
SDGs	United Nations Sustainable Development Goals
SIGI	Social Institutions and Gender Index
STEM	science, technology, engineering and mathematics
UBS	Union Bank of Switzerland
UN	United Nations
WBL	Women, Business and the Law
WHO	World Health Organization
WVS	World Values Survey

Executive summary

Masculinities are social constructs that relate to perceived notions – shared by both men and women – about how men behave and how they are expected to behave in order to be considered "real" men. They are shaped by and are part of social institutions – formal and informal laws, social norms and practices. Diverse forms of masculinities coexist across cultures, geographical locations and time, and some of these masculinities directly hinder women's empowerment and gender equality.

"Restrictive masculinities" and their associated norms are often rigid and promote inflexible notions and expectations of what it means to be a "real" man. In contrast, other masculinities, defined in this publication as "gender-equitable masculinities", present a more flexible alternative, permitting men to take on diverse roles and behaviours, while not limiting women's agency. For example, gender-equitable masculinities do not define men's role in the household as strictly providers, but rather allow for their fuller engagement in all aspects of household life, including unpaid care and domestic work. Furthermore, by acknowledging women's economic contribution, gender-equitable masculinities support women's broader access to education, the labour market and decision-making roles. Indeed, the masculinities that govern a society shape women's and girls' opportunities and constraints across all aspects of life, especially within the economic, political and private spheres.

This publication analyses norms of restrictive masculinities and provides a roadmap to measure changing norms of masculinities. It identifies ten norms of restrictive masculinities that produce direct consequences for women's and girls' empowerment and well-being across the economic, political and private spheres. It also provides an alternative vision of gender-equitable masculinities across these spheres. In order to facilitate gender-equitable masculinities that promote women's empowerment and provide support towards gender equality, there is a need to equip policy makers with the tools to facilitate this transformation. One of these tools is the ability to measure masculine norms across cultures and geographies. As such, this report proposes indicators that can be used as proxies to measure and analyse changing masculinities and their impact on women's empowerment.

Ten norms of restrictive masculinities that are directly obstructing women's empowerment

The public sphere, especially the **economic and political spheres**, has historically been the domain of men. Within this sphere, there are five norms that characterise restrictive masculinities and which are widely accepted across cultures. According to these norms, a "real" man should:

- **Be the breadwinner,** working for pay to provide for the material needs of the household.
- **Be financially dominant,** earning more than women.
- **Work in "manly" jobs,** regarding those professions that society defines as "men's work" and not those it views as "women's work".
- **Be the "ideal worker",** prioritising work over all other aspects of life.
- **Be a "manly" leader,** cultivating an assertive and space-occupying leadership style.

While the private or domestic sphere has traditionally been treated as the domain of women, restrictive masculinities promote male dominance within this sphere as well. In the **private sphere**, the five norms of restrictive masculinities entail that a "real" man should:

- **Have the final say in household decisions,** positioning him at the top of a hierarchy at home.
- **Control household assets,** solidifying his authority at home by controlling and administering household assets.
- **Protect and exercise guardianship of family members,** directing it especially at women and girls in the family.
- **Dominate sexual and reproductive choices,** initiating sexual encounters and making decisions regarding having children, birth spacing, etc.
- **Not do unpaid care and domestic work,** considering this work as generally "women's work".

These norms of restrictive masculinities induce direct negative consequences for women and girls. In the economic sphere, for example, these norms promote the devaluation of women's economic contribution and support the view that men's labour is more important and valuable than women's labour. As such, these norms justify women's exclusion from the labour force, high-status jobs and decision-making positions. In the political sphere, these norms uphold the view that leadership is a masculine characteristic and that men inherently make better leaders than women. In the private sphere, norms defining men's roles as decision makers minimise women's and girls' agency and decision-making power over their time, bodies and resources.

To facilitate social transformations towards gender-equitable masculinities, more data is key

It is increasingly clear that restrictive masculinities must be addressed in order to facilitate women's empowerment and gender equality. With the right tools, policy makers are well positioned to accelerate the transformation of masculine norms. Data on masculinities is one of these critical tools which can provide insight into the current state of masculine norms and allow policy makers to measure the impact that actions such as policies, legal reforms and campaigns have on masculinities. For instance, with the right data, policy makers can better understand the way norms of masculinities are influencing the low uptake of paternity leave. Equipped with this knowledge, they can create campaigns, national programmes and legal changes to address these norms and promote gender-equitable masculinities, especially when it comes to care. Furthermore, data on masculinities will enable a better knowledge of the role that large-scale phenomena, such as economic crises and the Covid-19 pandemic, play in shaping masculine norms. However, data on masculinities remain unevenly available and incomplete, thus preventing comparisons across countries, regions and time. As such, there is a need for greater investment in data collection. This publication proposes a set of indicators to guide future data collection efforts and an evidence-based approach to policy making.

1 What are masculinities?

This chapter introduces and defines masculinities. It clarifies the choice of terminology used throughout this publication. The chapter also defines the scope of the report, emphasising that while masculinities can and do harm men and boys, the focus of this research is the ways in which some masculine norms negatively affect women's empowerment. Finally, the chapter offers an overview of the report's structure.

Diverse forms of masculinity coexist across cultures, geographical locations and time. Masculinities are social constructions of "what it means to be a man" (Box 1.1), which vary with ethnicity, age and socio-economic background, among other factors (Kaufman, 1999[1]). Masculinities, part of social institutions themselves, can play an important role in upholding discriminatory social institutions – the laws, social norms and practices that perpetuate women's disempowerment and gender inequality. Masculinities, and gender norms in general, are learnt in early childhood and reinforced throughout one's life; nevertheless, they are subject to individual negotiation and choice (Waling, 2019[2]). Through individual agency, women and men can and do make different choices about their beliefs and expectations, internalising and adapting their perceptions of what it means to be a "real" man.[1]

Some masculinities can impede women's empowerment while others may support it. Restrictive masculinities[2] draw on a binary definition of gender and define men's roles and responsibilities as the opposite of women's, leading to a gender power imbalance (Connell, 1987[3])(Box 1.2). Even if very few men enact and embody all aspects of restrictive masculinities, their idealisation makes these dimensions widely normative (Connell and Messerschmidt, 2005[4]). Norms of restrictive masculinities coexist with other gender-equitable masculine norms, which can be compatible and even supportive of women's empowerment and gender equality (Barker, 2007[5]). In Brazil, for example, 43% of men believe that a man should have the final word about decisions in his home, while 53% believe that a woman's most important role is to take care of her home and cook (Barker et al., 2010[6]). This suggests strong support for the gender binary and patriarchal gender norms. However, the same individuals also exhibit gender-equitable norms: 90% believe that changing diapers, giving children a bath and feeding children are not only mothers' responsibilities, suggesting that they believe fathers should also engage in childcare (Barker et al., 2010[6]).

Box 1.1. Definition of masculinities

Masculinities encompass the various socially constructed ways of being and acting, values and expectations associated with being and becoming a man in a given society, location and temporal space. While masculinities are mostly linked with biological men and boys, they are not biologically driven and not only performed by men (OECD, 2019[7]).

Masculinities are social constructs. They are both shaped by and part of social institutions – formal and informal laws, social norms and practices. They relate to perceived notions, shared by both men and women, about how "real" men behave and, importantly, how men are expected to behave in specific settings in order to be considered "real" men. Masculinities are not innate or linked to biological maleness, but rather learnt through social interactions from early childhood into adolescence and adulthood, and transmitted from generation to generation (Schrock and Schwalbe, 2009[8]). Masculinities develop and operate at different levels, including the interpersonal, communal, institutional and societal levels.

Masculinities are diverse. Different masculinities exist across cultures, geographical locations and time periods but also within cultures and are informed by factors such as age, socio-economic background, race, and religion (Kaufman, 1999[1]). Recognising the diversity of masculinities highlights that men are not a homogeneous group and masculinities are not a "fixed, ahistorical entity" (Connell, 2014[9]).

Masculinities are hierarchically ordered according to their conformity to a masculine ideal. The extent to which men adhere to or reject an ideal set of dominant norms of masculinity influences their status in society (Connell, 1995[10]). Individuals who successfully live up to hegemonic ideals enjoy more power in society, thus generating a power imbalance between men and women and among men themselves (Waling, 2019[2]). Furthermore, men, in all of their diversity, experience power differently and often in a contradictory manner – both reaping the benefits of their privilege and experiencing "immense pain, isolation and alienation" as a result (Kaufman, 1999[1]).

Norms of masculinities can be understood as collectively shared social norms and social expectations about what men and boys do and what they ought to do (Mackie et al., 2015[11]). Social norms define what is typical (descriptive norms) and what is appropriate (injunctive norms) for members of a group (in this case men and boys) to do and be (Heise and Manji, 2016[12]). Some of the social practices that hold these norms in place are the approval or disapproval of others, which may include sanctions such as labelling, gossip, intimidation or violence (Mackie et al., 2015[11]). Individual attitudes, although not a perfect proxy, are often used as indicators of social norms (Cislaghi, Manji and Heise, 2017[13]), and are used as such throughout this publication along with data on social practices. The combination of both kinds of indicators is based on the idea that norms, once internalised, are enacted through people's behaviours and social practices.

Since the 1990s, research, programming and policy making have reflected increasing attention to masculinities. Academic research in psychology, sociology and anthropology has studied diverse masculinities and their related norms [see (Connell, 1995[10]; Morrell, 1998[14]), among others]. The key role of men as allies of women's empowerment has been acknowledged in international and regional agendas [the Beijing Declaration and Platform of Action (BPfA); the Convention on the Elimination of All Forms of Discrimination against Women (CEDAW); the 2030 Agenda for Sustainable Development and the Sustainable Development Goals (SDGs); and more], as well as in national gender strategies. Various stakeholders have promoted gender-transformative actions to enhance men's well-being and at the same time to promote women's empowerment and gender equality. Thousands of country-level programmes engaging men and boys as key agents of gender equality have been implemented, notably through the initiatives of Promundo, the International Center for Research on Women (ICRW) and the more than 600 non-governmental organisations (NGOs) of the MenEngage Alliance. These efforts have been aided by the development of surveys, including the International Men and Gender Equality Survey (IMAGES), which have offered evidence of these social norms and how they are among the promoters of harmful behaviours (Barker et al., 2011[15]).

Box 1.2. Terminology matters for efforts to transform restrictive masculinities

Transforming masculinities begins by using language that challenges the underlying premise of restrictive masculinities, a rigid gender binary. Rather than defining what constitutes a "real" man as the opposite of a "real" woman, the chosen terminology should refrain from relying on fixed gender roles. For this reason, this publication has selected terminology that is impact focused. Specifically, it recommends describing masculinities according to their potential effect: promoting women's empowerment and gender equality or encouraging men to develop beliefs, behaviours and attributes which undermine these goals.

In order to describe the relationship between masculinities and gender equality, various terms have emerged in public and academic debates to indicate whether masculinities are conducive or obstructive to women's empowerment and gender equality. Widely used dichotomous terms in this context are "toxic" versus "healthy" masculinities. Less symbolically charged terms include "traditional" as opposed to "progressive" masculinities and "negative" versus "positive" masculinities (OECD, 2019[7]). Other frequently used terms are "harmful masculinities" or "patriarchal masculinities" to describe expressions of masculinity that have adverse effects on women and men themselves. Policy discourses and academic papers have also referred to "gender-egalitarian" (OECD, 2019[7]) or "gender-equitable" versus "gender-inequitable" masculinities (Marcus, Stavropoulou and Archer-Gupta, 2018[16]). This publication has elected to use the following terminology:

- "Gender-equitable masculinities" describes masculinities that are supportive of women's empowerment and gender equality and that undermine patriarchal structures and unequal gender power dynamics.
- "Restrictive masculinities" describes masculinities that confine men to their traditional role as the dominant gender group, undermining women's empowerment and gender equality.

Beyond the adjectives used to describe masculinities, gendered language used to refer to activities, behaviours, etc. must also be addressed with care. Gendered language refers to wording such as "masculine", "feminine", "manly" and "womanly", to name examples present in this paper. In particular, the distinction between masculine and manly is critical. The term "manly", although often used synonymously with "masculine", can also be used normatively as defined by "having or denoting those good qualities traditionally associated with men" (Oxford University Press, 2020[17]). Conversely, "masculine" lacks this normative connotation and refers to "having qualities or appearance traditionally associated with men" (Oxford University Press, 2020[18]).

This publication identifies and investigates ten defining norms of restrictive masculinities across the public and private spheres that jeopardise women's empowerment. Some persistent notions of what a "real" man should be sustain the disempowerment of women and girls and underpin inequalities in unpaid care work, parenthood, access to economic opportunities and decision-making power. This notably includes social norms dictating that a "real" man should: i) be the breadwinner, ii) be financially dominant, iii) work in "manly" jobs, iv) be the "ideal worker", v) be a "manly" leader, vi) not do unpaid care and domestic work, vii) have the final say in household decisions, viii) control household assets, ix) protect and exercise guardianship of family members, and x) dominate sexual and reproductive choices (see Figure 1.1). Moreover, strategies to re-establish male dominance – including the use of violence – emerge, as some men feel threatened by women's increasing political and economic rights and empowerment (Kedia and Verma, 2019[19]).

Figure 1.1. The ten norms of restrictive masculinities

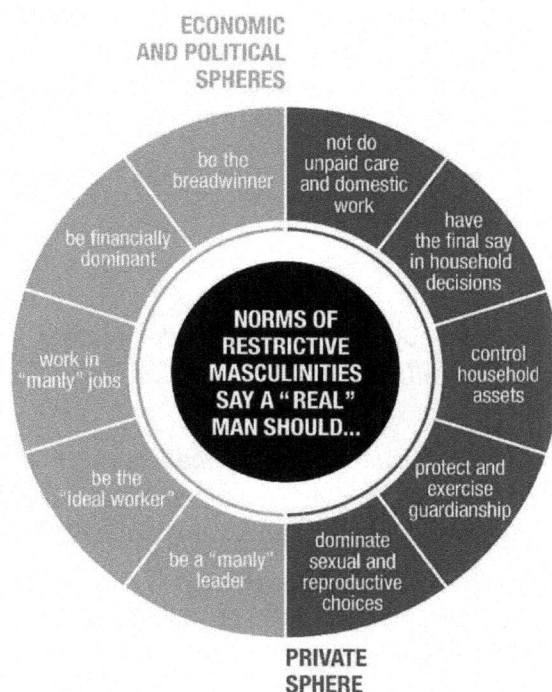

Note: This is not an exhaustive list of all norms of restrictive masculinities. The objective in the creation of this list was to account for those norms which have the most significant and direct impact on the empowerment of women and girls.
Source: Authors' elaboration.

This publication recognises the harm that restrictive masculinities do to men, but focuses specifically on their implications for women. Some men remain locked in the "man box"[3] as they feel pressure to conform to rigid gender norms, while those who do not comply with the dominant masculine ideals are further marginalised (Connell, 1995[10]; Heilman, Barker and Harrison, 2017[20]; Waling, 2019[2]). Dominant expressions of masculinities continue to hurt the physical and psychological health of both the men who conform to them and those who cannot (Kato-Wallace et al., 2016[21]). Together, men and women have much to gain from addressing restrictive masculinities. Shifting the norms of restrictive masculinities towards gender-equitable alternatives creates flexibility. For example, where gender-equitable norms are widely accepted, men who engage in childcare or take paternity leave are not stigmatised, and their wives/partners benefit from more equal divisions of unpaid care work, having time to pursue their careers or other interests. The norms of masculinities – whether restrictive or gender equitable – that dominate in societies have tremendous implications for women's empowerment in both the private and the economic and political spheres. This publication focuses on the norms of restrictive masculinities that directly impact the empowerment of women and girls. As such, these norms are most in need of attention from policy makers, who have the opportunity to address them.

After identifying ten norms of restrictive masculinities that require policy makers' attention, this report suggests indicators to track progress towards more gender-equitable masculinities. To address masculinities and promote women's empowerment, policy makers should be equipped with tools and indicators to: i) identify the norms of masculinities that are obstructive to gender equality, ii) design policies and programmes to address these norms, iii) track progress towards more gender-equitable norms and evaluate the efficiency of their actions, and, in doing so, iv) use this evidence to adjust their efforts. This implies measuring the impact of policies and programmes on women's lives, as well as the shift in both attitudes and behaviours of the whole population, not only of men and women who participate in specific programmes. This paper is organised as follows: Chapter 2 focuses on five norms of restrictive masculinities in the economic and political spheres, while Chapter 3 identifies five norms in the private sphere. Chapter 4 suggests indicators – both "ideal" indicators and available proxies – to track progress towards gender-equitable norms of masculinities within both spheres, and concludes with forward-looking ways this research can be mobilised, such as further data collection and policy analysis.

References

Barker, G. (2007), *The role of men and boys in achieving gender equality*, https://www.un.org/womenwatch/daw/public/w2000/W2000%20Men%20and%20Boys%20E%20web.pdf. [5]

Barker, G. et al. (2011), *Evolving Men: Initial Results from the International Men and Gender Equality Survey (IMAGES)*, https://www.icrw.org/wp-content/uploads/2016/10/Evolving-Men-Initial-Results-from-the-International-Men-and-Gender-Equality-Survey-IMAGES-1.pdf. [15]

Barker, G. et al. (2010), "Questioning gender norms with men to improve health outcomes: Evidence of impact", *Global Public Health*, Vol. 5(5), pp. 539-53, http://dx.doi.org/10.1080/17441690902942464. [6]

Cislaghi, B., K. Manji and L. Heise (2017), *Social Norms and Gender-Related Harmful Practices, Learning Report 2: Theory in support of better practice. Learning Group on Social Norms and Gender-Related Harmful Practices*, London School of Hygiene & Tropical Medicine, https://www.researchgate.net/publication/323075438_Social_norms_and_gender-related_harmful_practices_what_assistance_from_the_theory_to_the_practice. [13]

Connell, R. (2014), "The study of masculinities", *Qualitative Research Journal*, Vol. 14/1, pp. 5-15, https://www.researchgate.net/publication/275115285_The_study_of_masculinities. [9]

Connell, R. (1995), *Masculinities*, University of California Press, Berkeley. [10]

Connell, R. (1987), *Gender and Power: Society, the Person, and Sexual Politics*, Stanford University Press, Stanford. [3]

Connell, R. and J. Messerschmidt (2005), "Hegemonic Masculinity: Rethinking the Concept", *Gender and Society*, Vol. 19/6, pp. 829-859, http://www.jstor.org/stable/27640853. [4]

Heilman, B., G. Barker and A. Harrison (2017), *The Man Box: A Study on Being a Young Man in the US, UK, and Mexico*, https://promundoglobal.org/resources/man-box-study-young-man-us-uk-mexico/. [20]

Heise, L. and K. Manji (2016), *Social norms. GSDRC Professional Development*, https://www.researchgate.net/publication/338698501_Social_Norms. [12]

Kato-Wallace, J. et al. (2016), *Adolescent Boys and Young Men: Engaging Them as Supporters of Gender Equality and Health and Understanding their Vulnerabilities*, Promundo-US and UNFPA, Washington D.C., https://www.unfpa.org/sites/default/files/pub-pdf/Adolescent_Boys_and_Young_Men-SINGLE_PAGES-web.pdf. [21]

Kaufman, M. (1999), *Men, Feminism, and Men's Contradictory Experiences of Power*, Fernwood Books, Halifax, https://www.michaelkaufman.com/wp-content/uploads/2009/01/men_feminism.pdf. [1]

Kedia, S. and R. Verma (2019), *Gender norms and masculinities: a topic guide*, ALIGN, https://www.alignplatform.org/sites/default/files/2019-06/masculinities_guide_1.pdf. [19]

Mackie, G. et al. (2015), *What are social norms? How are they measured?*, University of California at San Diego-UNICEF Working Paper, http://globalresearchandadvocacygroup.org/wp-content/uploads/2018/06/What-are-Social-Norms.pdf. [11]

Marcus, R., M. Stavropoulou and N. Archer-Gupta (2018), *Programming with adolescent boys to promote gender-equitable masculinities*, https://www.odi.org/publications/11321-programming-adolescent-boys-promote-gender-equitable-masculinities-rigorous-review. [16]

Morrell, R. (1998), "Of boys and men: masculinity and gender in Southern African studies", *Journal of Southern African Studies*, Vol. 24/4, pp. 605-630, http://dx.doi.org/10.1080/03057079808708593. [14]

OECD (2019), "Engaging with men and masculinities in fragile and conflict-affected states", *OECD Development Policy Papers*, No. 17, OECD Publishing, Paris, https://dx.doi.org/10.1787/36e1bb11-en. [7]

Oxford University Press (2020), *Definition for masculine*, https://www.lexico.com/definition/masculine (accessed on 26 October 2020). [18]

Oxford University Press (2020), *Definition of manly*, https://www.lexico.com/about (accessed on 26 October 2020). [17]

Schrock, D. and M. Schwalbe (2009), "Men, Masculinity, and Manhood Acts", *Annual Review of Sociology*, Vol. 35/1, pp. 277-295, http://www.annualreviews.org/doi/10.1146/annurev-soc-070308-115933. [8]

Waling, A. (2019), "Problematising 'Toxic' and 'Healthy' Masculinity for Addressing Gender Inequalities", *Australian Feminist Studies*, Vol. 34/101, pp. 362-375, https://www.tandfonline.com/doi/pdf/10.1080/08164649.2019.1679021. [2]

Notes

[1] The term "real man" is used throughout this paper to denote the ideal man. While this ideal vision of manhood surely varies across contexts – both time and space – this report aims to highlight the similarities among these norms.

[2] This paper uses the term "restrictive masculinities" to describe masculinities that confine men to their traditional role as the dominant gender group, undermining gender equality; it uses the term "gender-equitable masculinities" to describe masculinities that are supportive of gender equality and that undermine patriarchal structures and unequal gender power dynamics. See Box 1.2 for discussion on the terminology.

[3] (Heilman, Barker and Harrison, 2017[20]) define the man box as "a rigid construct of cultural ideas about male identity".

2 Masculinities and women's empowerment in the economic and political spheres

This chapter presents five norms of restrictive masculinities that directly affect women's and girls' empowerment and well-being in the economic and political spheres. The norms in these spheres dictate that a "real" man should: i) be the breadwinner, ii) be financially dominant, iii) work in "manly" jobs, iv) be the "ideal worker" and v) be a "manly" leader. As such, these norms emphasise men's economic and leadership roles in society, which in turn promote the devaluation of women's contribution to these spheres. Even so, in some places, the masculine norms that characterise the political and economic spheres are not fully restrictive, demonstrating a growing acceptance of gender-equitable masculinities.

Introduction

Historically, patriarchal norms have defined the economic and political spheres as the domain of men. Across cultures, the traditional image of a powerful man was that of a public figure holding both political and economic power. Until the start of the 21st century, most positions of political leadership were occupied by men, including heads of states. By 2021, only 21 out of 195 countries[1] and territories listed by the United Nations (UN) are led by female heads of state or government (IPU Parline, 2020[1]). Similarly, leadership positions in business are dominated by men: in 2014, female chief executive officers (CEOs) led 5% of private sector companies in Africa, 2% in Latin America, 3% in Europe and 4% in Asia (McKinsey & Co, 2016[2]).

Political and economic power are pivotal in the social construction of restrictive masculinities. Ideals of dominance and power over both women and men are deeply embedded within restrictive masculinities (Connell, 1987[3]). Acquiring and maintaining political and economic power is a fundamental strategy to control other people – but resist being controlled by others – creating hierarchies among men and eliciting deference (Ezzell, 2016[4]; Schrock and Schwalbe, 2009[5]). On the one hand, political leadership comes with power and is premised on submission. On the other hand, financial dominance, competition and the projection of "success" are inherent to a dominant model of masculinity (Berdahl et al., 2018[6]; Bertrand, Kamenica and Pan, 2015[7]; Simpson, 2004[8]). This chapter discusses five norms of restrictive masculinities in the economic and political spheres that dictate that "real" men should: i) be the breadwinner, ii) be financially dominant, iii) work in "manly" jobs, iv) be the "ideal worker" and v) be a "manly" leader (Figure 2.1).

Figure 2.1. Defining norms of restrictive masculinities in the economic and political spheres

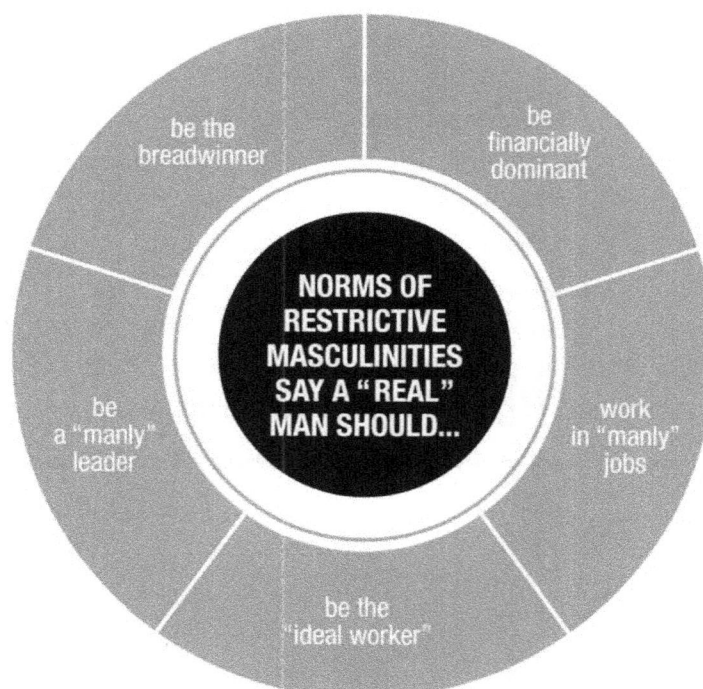

Source: Authors' elaboration.

Norms of restrictive masculinities in the economic and political spheres are detrimental to women's empowerment and well-being in various ways. First, social acceptance of such norms leaves little room for women's empowerment, as it confines women to their reproductive and caring roles and relies on the dominance of men in political and economic activities. This restricts women's participation in politics and in the labour market, justifies discriminatory practices towards working mothers, and limits the possibility of their (political and professional) career development and progression. Second, norms of restrictive masculinities may ascribe sons a higher economic value than daughters. In this regard, they reinforce the harmful and discriminatory practices embedded in son preference, leading to potentially lower investment in girls' education, unequal inheritance rights and missing women.[2] Third, restrictive masculinities spurn and downgrade what is feminine and what women value most. Thus, women ought to emulate men and conform to restrictive masculinities in order to succeed in political and economic activities. Finally, restrictive masculinities also put women at risk of violence at home, at work and in public spaces. Violence and sexual harassment can emerge when men sense a threat to their masculinity and a shift in the status quo that has favoured them in the past.

Gender-equitable masculinities that are supportive of women's political and economic empowerment are gaining prominence. Social change has started: legal reforms and gender-transformative programmes and policies are challenging the structures, beliefs, practices and institutions that used to sustain male privilege and dominance over women in the economic and political spheres (OECD, 2019[9]). For example, more and more women and men around the world are eager to see men participating more in childcare and domestic activities, and men themselves see the benefit of doing so. Similarly, acceptance of dual-earner couples as an alternative to the breadwinner/housekeeper model is more widespread, supporting a greater economic role for women. Finally, the value of diverse workplaces is gaining greater recognition in terms of financial returns, staff retention and job satisfaction, and more employers are taking steps to promote inclusive work environments (UN Women, 2019[10]).

This chapter is structured around five defining features of restrictive masculinities in the economic and political spheres. For each of these five defining features, this chapter investigates their consequences for women's empowerment and provides evidence of gender-equitable alternatives.

1. Norms of restrictive masculinities dictate that a "real" man should be the breadwinner

Across time, space and cultures, one of the most salient characteristics of being a "real" man lies in his role as a breadwinner and financial provider. Whether men bring food to the family table through paid employment, fishing or hunting, societies expect men to actively fulfil their families' fundamental needs. Consequently, masculinities are strongly associated with carrying out work and financially supporting their household (Mehta and Dementieva, 2017[11]; Zuo and Tang, 2000[12]). In Azerbaijan in 2016, for example, 53% and 48% of men and women, respectively, declared that a man who does not have an income is of no value (UNFPA/SCFWCA, 2018[13]). In Burkina Faso in 2017, 93% of the respondents declared that men should provide for their families in order to be perceived as "real" men (OECD, 2018[14]). In Ethiopia and Zimbabwe in 2020, 22% and 36% of the respondents, respectively, declared that men, not women, should really be the ones to bring home money to provide for the family (Haerpfer et al., 2020[15]). In the United States in 2017, almost three-quarters (71%) of respondents declared that men should support their family financially in order to be good husbands/partners. By comparison, only one-third (32%) of respondents had the same expectations of women (Parker and Stepler, 2017[16]). In 2017, across all 28 European Union (EU-28) countries, 43% of the respondents declared that the most important role of a man is to earn money, and up to 80% said the same in Bulgaria (Eurobarometer, 2017[17]).

Figure 2.2. Attitudes prioritising men's employment over women's are related to wide gaps in labour force participation

Female to male labour force participation ratio by the percentage of the population declaring that men should have more right to a job than women when jobs are scarce

Female to male labour force participation ratio

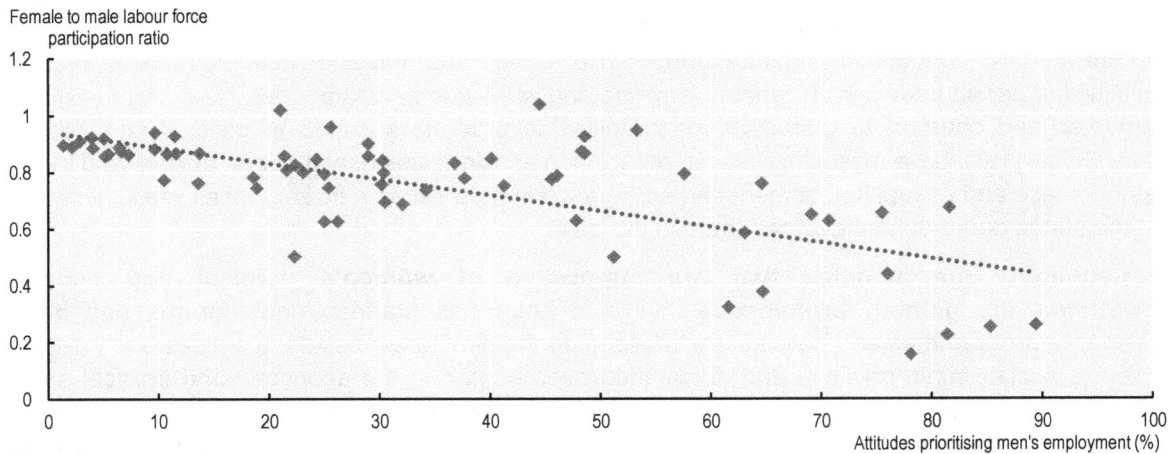

Attitudes prioritising men's employment (%)

Note: Attitudes prioritising men's employment are measured as the percentage of respondents agreeing or strongly agreeing with the statement "When jobs are scarce, men should have more right to a job than women". $R^2 = 0.4965$.
Source: (Haerpfer et al., 2020[15]), World Values Survey: Round Seven – Country-Pooled Datafile, http://www.worldvaluessurvey.org/WVSDocumentationWV7.jsp; (ILOStat, 2021[18]), Statistics on the working-age population and labour force, https://ilostat.ilo.org/topics/population-and-labour-force/.

StatLink 🔗 https://doi.org/10.1787/888934230395

If providing for the family is a man's prerogative according to restrictive masculinities, women have no critical role to play in the labour market. Social expectations towards men's role as breadwinners and financial providers restrict women's labour force participation and outcomes. In times of limited employment opportunities, such as those brought on by the Covid-19 pandemic, patriarchal social norms favour men's employment over women's. Indeed when lockdowns were imposed in Jordan, employers sent women employees home first to complete their domestic duties, and reports have shown that some companies have started to cut women's wages and/or benefits first (OECD, 2020[19]). Furthermore, in the 49 countries where data are available for the 2017-20 period, one in three respondents (33%) declared that men should have more right to a job than women when jobs are scarce, reaching more than three in four (75%) respondents in Bangladesh, Egypt, Indonesia, Iraq, Jordan, Myanmar and Pakistan (Haerpfer et al., 2020[15]). Moreover, in Burkina Faso in 2017, for example, seven out of ten respondents declared that it is more difficult for women to find a formal job, because of her gender (OECD, 2018[14]). One of the consequences of women's limited opportunities to join the labour market is that, very often, one of the only available entry points is the informal sector which offers lower pay and less social protection. Indeed, widespread support for patriarchal gender roles is correlated with lower female labour force participation and employment rates (Figure 2.2). In 2019 at the global level, 47% of women of working-age were in the labour force and 45% were employed, compared with 74% and 70% of men, respectively (ILOSTAT, 2020[20]). This norm of restrictive masculinities is also correlated with other gender gaps in labour market outcomes, such as higher rates of informal labour and vulnerability of women's employment, lower female earnings, and both vertical and horizontal gender segregation at work.[3]

Expectations towards men's role as breadwinner and financial provider are reflected in the perceived higher economic value of sons. In some contexts, men are expected to financially support their family, not only as husbands and partners but also as sons; in such settings, a son's wealth matters more to households than a daughter's, explaining the higher economic value associated with sons (Gill and Mitra-Kahn, 2009[21]). This is especially the case in some patriarchal rural societies, where adult sons are expected to provide for their parents, and this expectation is particularly strong where access to pensions and social protection is limited. Indeed, evidence from India shows that greater acceptance of the norms of restrictive masculinities is related to a greater preference for sons over daughters (Nanda et al., 2014[22]). The impact of beliefs of a son's greater economic value, tied to the view that "real" men are breadwinners, adversely affects women's opportunities, especially in education.

The greater economic role of sons can negatively affect girls' access to education. When resources are scarce, the higher economic value associated with sons might lead to lower investment in daughters' education as parents believe they do not directly benefit from daughters' returns on schooling (Foster and Rosenzweig, 1999[23]). In the 17 countries where data are available for 2019, between 7% of female respondents in New Zealand and Tunisia and 30% in India declared having had difficulty accessing education and professional training as compared with their male peers/ or relatives (Focus 2030 and Women Deliver, 2021[24]). Attitudes are also an important factor guiding whether, and to what extent, girls are encouraged to pursue educational opportunities and are supported in doing so. In this regard, many people still think higher education is less important for girls than boys. In the 49 countries where data are available for the 2017-20 period, on average almost one in five (20%) respondents declared that university is more important for boys than for girls, and more than one in three (33%) did so in Bangladesh, Indonesia, Islamic Republic of Iran (hereafter "Iran"), Korea, Kyrgyzstan, Malaysia, Myanmar, Nigeria, Pakistan, the Philippines and Tajikistan (Haerpfer et al., 2020[15]).

Similarly, biased expectations towards sons' roles as providers can have wide consequences on girls' empowerment and well-being. This includes unequal inheritance rights between boys and girls as well as discriminatory social practices governing the inheritance of land and non-land assets (Bhalotra, Brulé and Roy, 2017[25]; OECD, 2019[9]). Property, and in particular land, is a critical determinant of economic and social status in many places. This is especially true when sons tend to co-reside with parents and work on the land, contribute to wealth creation as well as old-age security, and subsequently inherit the land (Bhalotra, Brulé and Roy, 2017[25]; Botticini and Siow, 2003[26]). Son preference and daughter devaluation can also manifest in sex-selective abortions and multiple forms of neglect, including breastfeeding duration, immunisation and nutrition (Jayachandran and Kuziemko, 2011[27]; Oster, 2009[28]). One of the most striking illustrations of son preference is the "missing women" phenomenon: the shortfall in the number of women relative to the expected number of women in a region or country (Miller, 1981[29]; Sen, 1990[30]).

The greater inclusion of women in the labour force is challenging restrictive expectations towards men's role as breadwinners. In both developed and developing countries, women's employment rates have increased over the last decades and fewer households have an economic model relying on a single earner, traditionally the man (ILO, 2018[31]). In most Organisation for Economic Co-operation and Development (OECD) member countries, for example, fewer than one in three couples with at least one child have a man working 40 or more hours per week and a woman not engaging in paid work; this figure drops to one in ten couples in Belgium, Denmark, France, Norway and Sweden (OECD, 2016[32]). Norms of masculinities are evolving to be more gender equitable alongside economic needs (Bolzendahl and Myers, 2004[33]; Brewster and Padavic, 2000[34]; Waismel-Manor, Levanon and Tolbert, 2016[35]). Data show a wider acceptance of men having an economically active wife. Similarly, men seem to be "allowed" not to be the breadwinner and still be considered "real" men. In the United States, for example, acceptance of working mothers, equal roles for women in the workplace, dual-income families, and fathers working half-time or stay-at-home dads has increased between the 1970s and the 2010s (Donnelly et al., 2015[36]). Indeed, support for a husband working half-time and stay-at-home dads has more than doubled from the

1970s to the 2010s – from 25% to 66% and 17% to 41%, respectively (Donnelly et al., 2015[36]) Similarly, fewer respondents supported the single, male-earner structure (29% in the 2010s compared with 40% in the 1970s), while more supported the dual-earner structure (77% in the 2010s compared with 62% in the 1970s) (Donnelly et al., 2015[36]).

Gender-equitable masculinities acknowledge women's economic contribution and therefore support their greater access to education and the labour market, as employees and entrepreneurs. Worldwide, 83% of women and 77% of men declared that it is perfectly acceptable for any woman in their family to have a paid job outside the home if she wants one (Gallup, 2017[37]). As a result of women's greater inclusion in the labour market, more and more households are becoming financially dependent on women (Zuo and Tang, 2000[12]). In the United States in 1970, the male partner contributed more than 60% of the couple's earnings in three-quarters of families with a dual-earner economic structure (Raley, Mattingly and Bianchi, 2006[38]). In 2000, almost one-half of dual-earner couples were equal earners, with each partner contributing between 40% and 60% of total household income, or had the female partner as the primary earner (Raley, Mattingly and Bianchi, 2006[38]).

2. Norms of restrictive masculinities dictate that a "real" man should be financially dominant

With the increasing number of dual-earner couples, women's improving economic status may be viewed as a challenge to male dominance in the economic and public spheres. As indicated previously, women's increasing political and economic empowerment has eroded the foundation of at least one norm of restrictive masculinities: that men be the breadwinners and financial providers for their households (Bernard, 1993[39]; Goode, 1994[40]). Meanwhile, women's access to political and economic leadership roles showcases their ability to exercise power over men and other women. In this context, financial dominance may emerge as fundamental for re-establishing male dominance.

Financial dominance, in which men earn more than women, is demonstrated in practice through gender pay gaps. In 2017, the global gender pay gap was 22% (ILO, 2018[41]). Furthermore progress to close the gender pay gap has been slow and uneven. For example, among the 19 G20 countries, the gender pay gap narrowed in only six countries between 2017 and 2019 (OECD, 2020[42]). Moreover, in the 17 countries where data are available for 2019, a range of between 13% of female respondents in Tunisia and 37% in Switzerland declared that they were not being paid as much as their male colleagues (Focus 2030 and Women Deliver, 2021[24]). The view that "real" men are financially dominant is tied to acceptance of pay gaps. In India in 2019 for example, 35% of respondents found it acceptable that women earn less than men for the same work. Most importantly, this support for gender inequalities does not vary between women and men and is higher among the working-age population (25-49 years: 40%) than among older respondents (60 years and older: 11%) (Focus 2030 and Women Deliver, 2021[24]).

The belief that "real" men are financially dominant is related to pay discrimination. First, restrictive gender norms are internalised by both women and men. Among women, this may lead some to unconsciously limit themselves and their aspirations, moreover it may drive the conscious decision not to negotiate their pay or ask for a raise (Barron, 2003[43]). Meanwhile among men, the belief that "real" men are financially dominant may have the opposite effect, encouraging them to ask for raises and negotiate their pay. These norms are also internalised by decision makers in the workplace and inform both the conscious and unconscious biases of employers. For example, an employer who has internalised the view that men are the breadwinners and should be financially dominant may also view women's wages as supplementary to the household. This may in turn lead them to favour men and discriminate against women when it comes to pay or positions. While ways these norms inform men's and women's experiences and choices are not enough to explain persistently wide gender pay gaps, they may help to illuminate the part of the gender pay gap that is not well explained by widely recognised factors such as vertical and horizontal labour force segregation.

Women's greater educational outcomes and gender-equitable policies alone are not enough to fix the gender imbalances at the top levels of business or gender pay gaps. In 2017, women were better educated than ever and were surpassing men in tertiary education in all regions but Africa, representing 53% of the world's tertiary graduates, from 48% in Africa to 59% in the Americas (UNESCO, 2018[44]). Moreover, almost 75% of enterprises worldwide have equal opportunity or diversity and inclusion policies in place (ILO, 2019[45]). However, women's representation in top positions in business still lags behind that of men and gender wage gaps are pervasive. Between 1991 and 2018, women held from 36% of management positions in North American countries to 10% in the Middle East and North Africa (MENA) region (ILO, 2019[46]). Globally in 2017, 13% of companies had no women on their boards, 30% of them had less than 10% of women board members, and 21% had between 11% and 29% of women board members (ILO, 2018[31]). Furthermore, the gender pay gap does not disappear when women are promoted to managerial roles: in 43 of the 93 countries for which data are available, the gender pay gap was indeed higher for managers than for all employees in 2019 (ILO, 2020[47]).[4]

Financial dominance as a norm of restrictive masculinities is also evident in the home. A powerful part of this restrictive norm is that "a man should earn more than his wife" (Akerlof and Kranton, 2000[48]). This notably translates into high aversion to the situation in which a wife out-earns her husband (Bertrand, Kamenica and Pan, 2015[7]). In the 49 countries where data are available for the 2017-20 period, nearly 37% of respondents declared that if a woman earns more money than her husband, it is almost certain to cause problems, surpassing 50% in Bangladesh, Plurinational State of Bolivia (hereafter "Bolivia"), Egypt, Iran, Jordan, Kyrgyzstan, Mexico, Myanmar, Nigeria, Pakistan and Zimbabwe (Figure 2.3) (Haerpfer et al., 2020[15]). Furthermore, in Ukraine, 37% of men declared that a man who earns less than his wife is of no value, demonstrating the strength of the aversion to this situation and the way in which it is viewed as emasculating (UNFPA Ukraine, 2018[49]).

Figure 2.3. In many countries there is significant aversion to women out-earning their husband

Percentage of respondents declaring that it is almost certain to cause problems if a woman earns more money than her husband

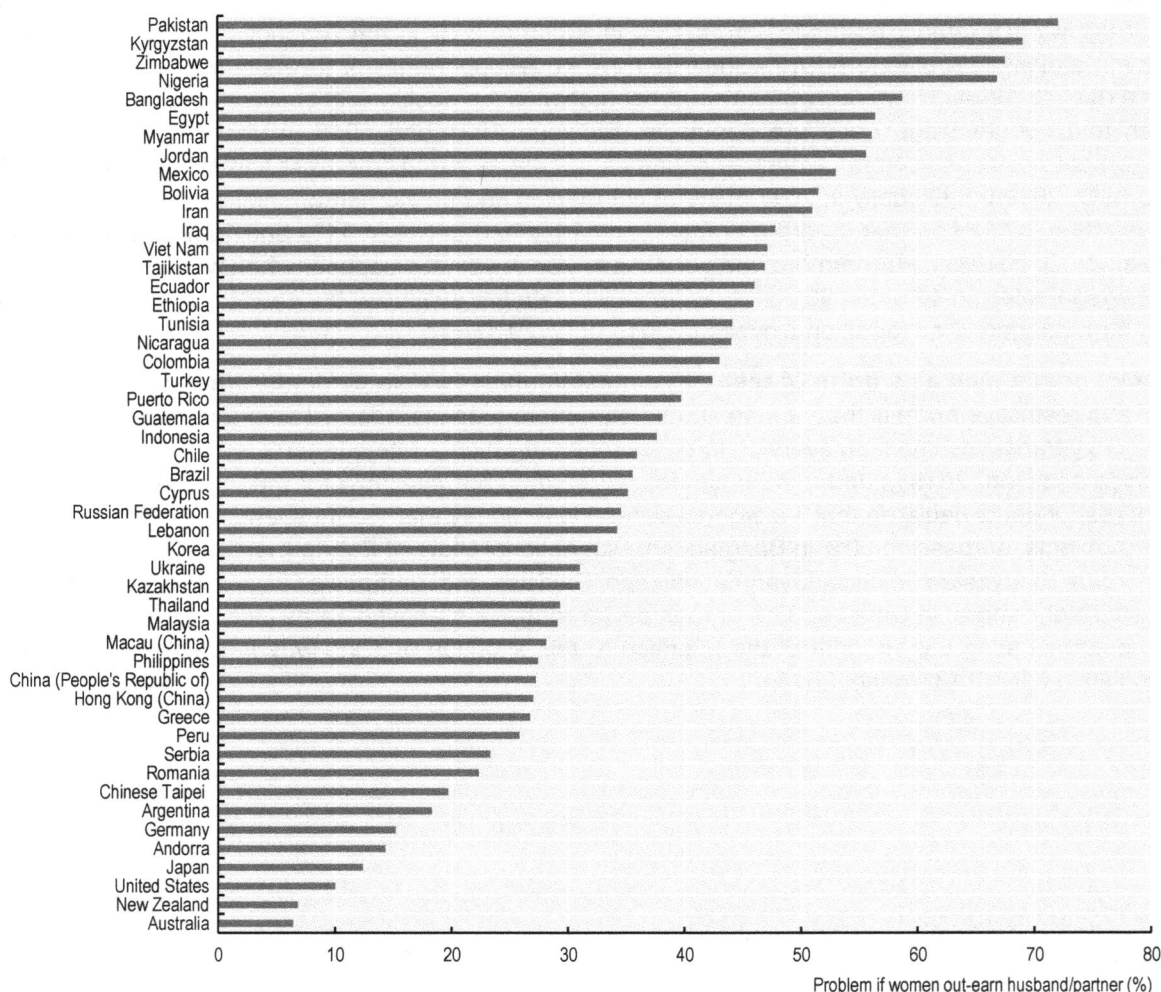

Note: Problem if women out-earn husband/partner refers to the percentage of respondents declaring that it is almost certain to cause problems if a woman out-earns her husband.
Source: (Haerpfer et al., 2020[15]), World Values Survey: Round Seven – Country-Pooled Datafile, http://www.worldvaluessurvey.org/WVSDocumentationWV7.jsp.

StatLink 🔗 https://doi.org/10.1787/888934230414

Norms of restrictive masculinities related to men's financial dominance induce consequences for women in the private sphere. Being financially dominant might lead to unequal bargaining and decision-making power within the household, to the disadvantage of women (Browning and Chiappori, 1998[50]; Lundberg and Pollak, 2008[51])(see Chapter 3, Section 2). Moreover, some strategies that are obstructive to gender equality may be implemented to re-establish male dominance at home and compensate for deviance from restrictive norms of masculinities. When wives out-earn their husbands, the men-breadwinner/women-homemaker gender norm is violated, creating tensions between spouses and pressure to compensate for such deviance by enacting a more traditional division of household labour

(Waismel-Manor, Levanon and Tolbert, 2016[35]). Men living with partners who earn higher wages than they do, tend to reduce the time they allocate to household chores as a response to this "gender deviance" (Bertrand, Kamenica and Pan, 2015[7]) (see Chapter 3, Section 1).

Restrictive masculinities promote the view that men who lack income and work are not "real" men, which threatens the well-being of men themselves and can lead to violence against women. The emphasis on men's financial dominance promotes the idea that a man's worth is directly associated with his economic status. This emphasis is a source of stress for many men and can drive them to migrate for work, and can lead to feelings of shame and frustration in times of economic hardship including periods of unemployment or underemployment. For example, research in India revealed that in 2009 nearly 28% of surveyed men reported feeling stressed or depressed because they did not have enough work, and 30% said they felt ashamed to face their families due to their employment status (Barker et al., 2010[52]). Moreover, evidence shows that economic stress can increase the prevalence of violence among men, both towards themselves through self-harm and violence against others, especially female partners (Barker et al., 2011[53]). Indeed the men who reported work related stress and shame, in the aforementioned survey, were 50% more likely to have committed violence against their female partners than men who did not report having such emotions (Barker et al., 2010[52]).

Violence can emerge as a reaction to shifting status quos that have previously favoured men and reinforced male dominance, especially in the economic sphere. Despite an increasing awareness that women's empowerment benefits both women and men, some people continue to view it as a synonym of men's disempowerment (Silberschmidt, 2001[54]). Some men who perceive women's empowerment as a threat to masculinity may adopt strategies and behaviours that harm women in order to re-establish male dominance and power. In the workplace and in public spaces, this might include sexual harassment and physically aggressive displays (Berdahl, 2007[55]; Bosson et al., 2009[56]; McLaughlin, Uggen and Blackstone, 2012[57]). In the home, domestic violence may also be perceived as a strategy to restore gender status when it has been threatened, leading to increased incidence and prevalence of intimate partner violence (Atkinson, Greenstein and Lang, 2005[58]; Bhattacharya, 2015[59]; Caridad Bueno and Henderson, 2017[60]; Finnoff, 2012[61]).

Policies and discourses promoting equal pay for equal work open new avenues for gender-equitable norms of masculinities. The International Labour Organization (ILO) Convention No. 100, establishing the principle of equal remuneration for work of equal value, has been translated into national legal frameworks. Of the 180 countries covered by the Social Institutions and Gender Index (SIGI) 2019, 166 have ratified the Convention and 148 have introduced legislation on equal remuneration for work of equal value; 27 countries legally require companies to report on how they pay women and men and 20 impose penalties for companies in cases of gender discrimination in recruitment and promotions (OECD, 2019[9]). Under the 2008 Swedish Discrimination Act, for example, employers must conduct remuneration surveys every three years and companies with more than 25 employees are obliged to draw up an action plan for equal pay for equal work on the basis of the surveys (OECD, 2019[9]). In addition, both men and women support gender equality in pay. In the EU-28 in 2017, for example, 90% of the population thought it was unacceptable that in some circumstances a woman would be paid less than a male colleague for the same job; this figure grows to more than 95% in France, Luxembourg, the Netherlands and Sweden (Eurobarometer, 2017[17]).

3. Norms of restrictive masculinities dictate that a "real" man should work in "manly" jobs

"Real" men work in "manly" jobs. Another important dimension of restrictive masculinities in the economic sphere is related to the type of work men should engage in. Gender norms play a crucial role in promoting and sustaining the social definition of tasks as either "men's work" or "women's work" (Simpson,

2004[8]). These social definitions not only correspond to which gender typically does these jobs, but also to gendered associations about the traits that make one suited for the work (Buscatto and Fusulier, 2014[62]). For example, some jobs are viewed as more suitable for men, such as fishers, heavy truck drivers, masons and carpenters, and may be linked to the belief that physical strength is a masculine trait, while others are seen as more appropriate for women, such as midwives, nurses and housekeepers, as being caring and attentive of others is typically viewed as a feminine trait. As such, working in "manly" jobs allows men to express their manhood, while working in "feminine" jobs is seen as an infringement of their dominant masculine identity. The man who moves into "women's work" risks compromising the perception that he is a "real" man and attracting suspicion and stigmatisation, even though he may also benefit professionally based on his gender relative to women in the same job (Buscatto and Fusulier, 2014[62]).

Legal frameworks may reinforce common understandings of which jobs are "manly" jobs. For example, by restricting women's access to some jobs and sectors – because they are deemed too dangerous or inappropriate for women – laws reinforce the gender binary and norms of restrictive masculinities. Among the 180 countries covered by the SIGI in 2019, 88 had legal frameworks prohibiting women from entering certain professions, while in 51 countries women could not legally work the same night hours as men (OECD, 2019[9]).

The gender binary and the related dichotomous definitions of jobs reinforce gender segregation and gaps in labour and educational outcomes. This partially explains both vertical and horizontal gender segregation at work – notably men's under-representation in "feminine" jobs (Figure 2.4) – and gender wage gaps, as "manly" jobs are also more remunerative. Moreover, it can lead to lower participation of women and girls in science, technology, engineering and mathematics (STEM) education programmes, for example. Norms of masculinities not only influence boys' choices but also those of girls, by defining what is appropriate for girls to do and through a role model effect (OECD, 2019[63]; OECD, 2015[64]; UNESCO, 2017[65]). The OECD's Programme for International Student Assessment (PISA) 2018 reveals that students aged 15 years have likely already internalised social messages about gender and jobs. For example, across all 79 countries surveyed, only 1% of girls reported wanting to work in information and communication technology (ICT) compared with 8% of boys (OECD, 2019[63]). Furthermore, among the high-achieving students in science and mathematics in 22 countries, the gender gap in expectations of working as an engineer was significant, standing higher than 15 percentage points (OECD, 2019[63]).

Figure 2.4. Gender segregation by occupation is significant

Percentage of employment by sex and occupation

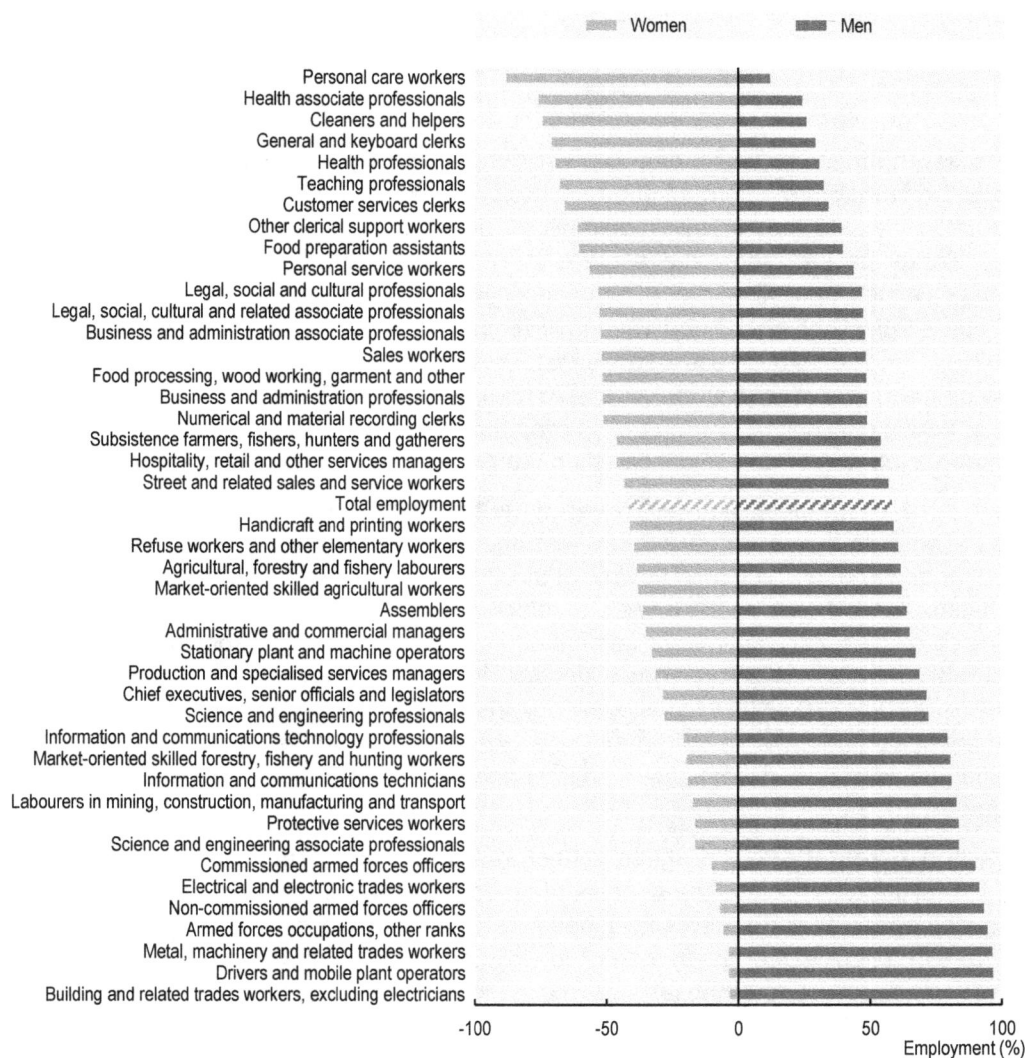

Note: Classification of occupations follows the International Standard Classification of Occupations (ISCO) 08 at the 2-digit level. Data are calculated as the weighted average for 121 countries using the latest year available.
Source: (ILOSTAT, 2020[20]), Labour statistics on women, https://ilostat.ilo.org/topics/women/.

StatLink https://doi.org/10.1787/888934230433

Women working in "manly" jobs and sectors may face a greater risk of violence. While it may be easier for women to enter into "manly" jobs than vice versa as working in "manly" jobs is still reconcilable with feminine identity, women who do so may find themselves at greater risk of gender-based violence (Simpson, 2004[8]; Williams, 1993[66]). As indicated previously, psychological, physical and sexual violence may be a way for some men to react to perceived threats to their masculine identity (Cross and Bagilhole, 2002[67]; Simpson, 2004[8]). This could notably be the case when women's job growth is influenced by employment in male-dominated fields. Women working in "manly" jobs may be subjected to moral and sexual harassment, as well as physical and sexual violence (Dahl, Vescio and Weaver, 2015[68]). Moreover, some women are increasingly perceived to have traditionally "manly" characteristics, such as being competitive, daring, adventurous and aggressive (Diekman and Eagly, 2000[69]). Some men might perceive such erosion of gender differences in work attitudes and behaviours as threats to their masculinity, and react aggressively (Dahl, Vescio and Weaver, 2015[68]).

4. Norms of restrictive masculinities dictate that a "real" man should be the "ideal worker"

Restrictive masculinities at work can be expressed through contests among men to prove themselves to be "real" men (Berdahl et al., 2018[6]). The workplace is a major site for the construction and reconstruction of what it means to be a man, as a crucial part of gender socialisation (Morgan, 1992[70]). As such, the workplace can constitute a place in which men attempt to secure their manhood and dominance over women and other men. Dominance over others is notably achieved by having relative control over valued physical, social and economic resources, including money and influence (Fiske and Berdahl, 2007[71]). Traditional business cultures foster restrictive norms of masculinities by rewarding "real" men with status and resources (Berdahl et al., 2018[6]). Indeed, in 2019, among the four countries with available data, nearly one-half of all men (49%) reported believing that being "manly/masculine" can help them get or keep a job, while 43% said it can help them get a pay rise (Ipsos, 2019[72]).

Characteristics of the "ideal worker" overlap with norms of restrictive masculinities. Being "feminine" is the antithesis of the "ideal worker" who should show no weakness, demonstrate strength and put work first (Mahalik et al., 2003[73]; Levant et al., 2010[74]). The latter notably means that the "ideal worker" is available to work long hours, travel and relocate (Heppner, 2013[75]). Moreover, the "ideal worker" allows nothing to come before their work commitments, including family responsibilities (Williams, Blair-Loy and Berdahl, 2013[76]). Whatever one's gender, in such settings success requires conforming to extreme masculine stereotypes. It includes being dominant, aggressively competitive, dedicated (i.e. being available continuously and full-time, and prioritising work over private life) and successful, and exhibiting toughness and avoiding "soft" or feminine emotions and behaviour (Mahalik et al., 2003[73]; Levant et al., 2010[74]; Heppner, 2013[75]).

Family-work and parental leave policies reflect restrictive masculinities. The lack of family-work policies and the failure to recognise the benefits of other forms of child-related leave than maternity leave reinforce the perception that men should behave as the "ideal worker". Only 91 of the 180 countries covered by the SIGI in 2019 offer paid paternity leave (OECD, 2019[9]). Moreover, even when paternity or parental leave schemes exist, few men take leave and the length of leave for mothers and fathers replicates traditional gender roles (OECD, 2019[9]) (see Chapter 3, Section 1). In the OECD, for example, women may benefit on average from 55.4 weeks of paid maternity or parental leave. This figure drops to eight weeks for father-specific leave (OECD, 2016[77]).

Women cannot be the "ideal worker", even if they conform to restrictive masculinities. The gender binary drives the assumption that female workers are less performant than men due to the mismatch between feminine attributes and those of the "ideal worker", especially in masculine gender-typed positions and roles. Employers' beliefs are strongly embedded in both descriptive gender stereotypes – what women and men are like – and prescriptive gender stereotypes – what women and men should be like – whatever their own gender (Heilman, 2012[78]). Many employers assume that male candidates are more likely to prioritise work over family life. They also expect women to take primary responsibility for childcare and the other needs of maintaining a home for their families. Gender stereotypes give rise to biased judgements and decisions, reinforcing the glass ceiling and impeding women's advancement and career progression due to gender-based discrimination in the recruitment process (Heilman, 2012[78]). In the 17 countries where data are available for 2019, a range of between 14% of female respondents in Tunisia and 39% in South Africa declared not having the same access to promotional opportunities in their job as their male peers (Focus 2030 and Women Deliver, 2021[24]). Whatever her marital status, a female worker is often perceived as less than "ideal", as it is assumed that at some point in her life family will take precedence over work (Williams, 2001[79]).

5. Norms of restrictive masculinities dictate that a "real" man should be a "manly" leader

Societies worldwide often associate leadership with restrictive masculinities (Holmes, 2006[80]). Not only are men expected to be (political and economic) leaders but also to lead in a "manly" way (Dahl, Vescio and Weaver, 2015[68]). Indeed, in many places, male leaders are often accused of not being "manly" enough. "Manly" leadership is characterised as competitive, tough, aggressive and space occupying (Poynting and Donaldson, 2005[81]). Such social expectations prompt "real" men to compete, to dominate others in the economic and public spheres and to face down opponents in situations of conflict, while also defining social understandings of what it means to be strong (Connell et al., 1982[82]). In Norway, for example, interviews with business students show that the male business leaders of tomorrow upheld traditional business masculinities while expressing more gender-equitable attitudes when societal issues were at stake (Halvorsen and Ljunggren, 2020[83]).

Legal reforms are necessary but are not sufficient on their own to foster social change. In all countries[5] but one ranked in the SIGI in 2019, women have the same rights as men to hold public and political office in the parliament, the public administration and the government (OECD, 2019[9]). To promote women's political empowerment and shift gender norms, 111 countries have also instituted measures to promote women's political participation, such as quotas or incentives for political parties to include women on candidate lists (OECD, 2019[9]). Nevertheless, social norms questioning women's ability to lead are still widespread and women are still under-represented in leadership positions (OECD, 2019[9]).

Men are often considered natural leaders, to the disadvantage of women (Eagly, 2004[84]). According to the expression "Think manager – think male", women are not expected to make effective leaders (Schein et al., 1996[85]). Throughout history, gender norms have promoted the idea that women are too kind and caring to be leaders (Ibarra and Obodaru, 2009[86]). For example, in the People's Republic of China (hereafter "China"), Germany, Japan, the United Kingdom and the United States, business students associated male managers with successful management (Schein, 2007[87]). In countries where data are available, 36% of respondents declared that men make better business executives, while 41% stated that men make better political leaders than women do (Haerpfer et al., 2020[15]). Such support for restrictive understandings of masculinities limits women's access to both political and economic leadership. A higher share of the population supporting restrictive gender roles is associated with lower representation of women in both political and economic leadership (Figure 2.5).

Women leaders suffer from being women. First, women ought to emulate men to succeed as leaders because successful managers are understood to possess characteristics more commonly ascribed to men (Booysen and Nkomo, 2007[88]). In the 27 countries where data are available, 17% of respondents declared that they would feel uncomfortable if their boss were a woman (Ipsos, 2019[89]). Moreover, in Burkina Faso, 59% of respondents declared it easier to work under the supervision of a male rather than a female boss (OECD, 2018[14]). Second, as identified earlier, there are more men in top corporate positions than women, which makes them the standard while women remain the exception. Being perceived as an exception or a token makes women stand out, and all of their actions are scrutinised and analysed much more frequently, increasing the pressure they bear at work (Oakley, 2000[90]). Not only do women have to conform to restrictive masculinities to prove themselves but they also have to do twice as much as men do for the same recognition. In the United States, for example, about 40% of respondents point to a double standard for women seeking to climb to the highest levels of either politics or business, where they have to do more than men to prove themselves (Pew Research Center, 2015[91]). Third, women political and economic leaders have to endure prejudiced comments ranging from (moral and sexual) harassment to personal insults – often associated with stereotypes and motherhood (Hryniewicz and Vianna, 2018[92]). Finally, women entrepreneurs may face difficulties in hiring employees. In Burkina Faso, for example, about 70% of respondents declared it easier to recruit for male employers than for female employers (OECD, 2018[14]).

Figure 2.5. Women's political representation is negatively correlated with attitudes indicating a wide acceptance of restrictive masculinities related to political leadership

Women's representation in parliaments by percentage of the population declaring that men make better political leaders than women do, 2020

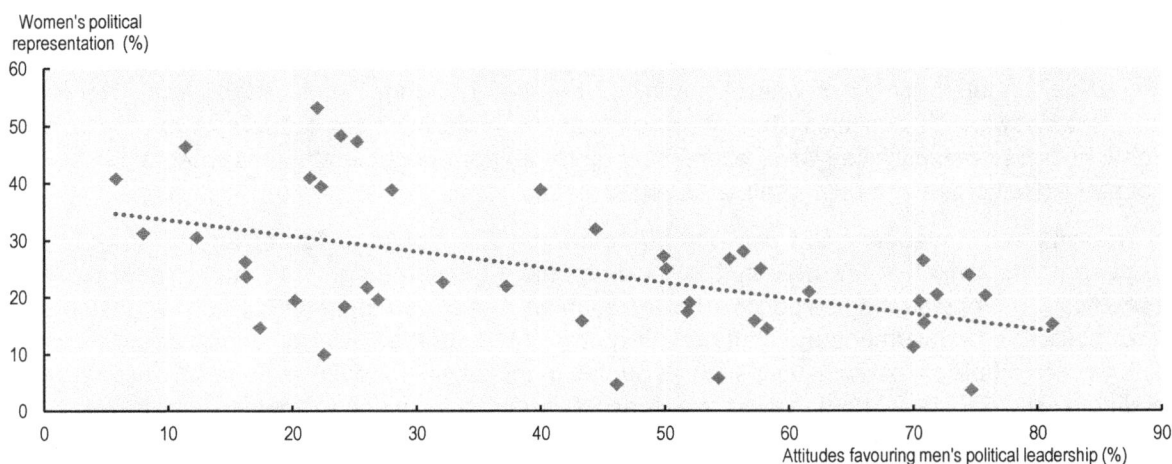

Note: Women's political representation refers to the percentage of women parliamentarians/representatives within the single/lower house of parliament/legislature. Attitudes favouring the political leadership of men refers to the percentage of respondents that agree/strongly agree that "on the whole, men make better political leaders than women do". R^2=0.264.
Source: (Haerpfer et al., 2020[15]), World Values Survey: Round Seven – Country-Pooled Datafile, http://www.worldvaluessurvey.org/WVSDocumentationWV7.jsp; (IPU Parline, 2020[1]), Monthly ranking of women in national parliaments, https://data.ipu.org/women-ranking?month=7&year=2020 (accessed on 4 February 2021).

StatLink https://doi.org/10.1787/888934230452

Given the widespread belief that leadership is a masculine attribute, some women underestimate their own leadership abilities. On the supply side, the correlation between women's under-representation in leadership positions and norms of restrictive masculinities may be explained by the fact that women refrain from applying for and pursuing leadership positions. Women and girls may internalise discriminatory beliefs, which shape their own identity, aspirations and behaviours. For example, in the United Kingdom in 2018, more than one-half of girls aged 7-10 years wanted to be leaders in their chosen job, but the numbers fell among those aged 11-21 years (Girlguiding, 2018[93]). One reason for this could be a reluctance to face the same challenges they see current women leaders facing. One in three girls puts off going into politics because of the way female politicians are treated, while one in four believed there are fewer women business leaders because women are treated less fairly than men (Girlguiding, 2018[93]).

Recruitment processes are also influenced by norms of restrictive masculinities. On the demand side, employers and voters also make their choices based on beliefs that may include that men make better leaders. They may therefore be less likely to choose or elect women into economic and political leadership positions, whatever their own gender. These conscious and unconscious biases lead to decisions in favour of men and to the detriment of women, and naturally creep into the economic and public spheres (McCormick-Huhn, Kim and Shields, 2019[94]; Wynn and Correll, 2018[95]). Even female and male scientists at Yale University, who are trained to reject the subjective, were more likely to hire men, rank them higher in competency than women, and pay them USD 4 000 more per year than women (Moss-Racusin et al., 2012[96]).

Increasing evidence of successful women leaders is promoting more gender-neutral perceptions of leadership. Observation has unconscious effects on perception (Halász and Cunnington, 2012[97]). The behaviour observed in some current leaders – who demonstrate humility, discipline, concentration and good communication; are not egocentric; and have a discreet personality – goes against the traditional idea of an efficient leader who is charismatic, selfish, strong-willed and also a man (Williams, 2005[98]). This shows that a leader can be successful without being a man or conforming to restrictive masculinities. As a result, social expectations of leadership are evolving "from the all-male leadership concept to a mix of male and female behaviours that can form a better leader" (Hryniewicz and Vianna, 2018[92]). Indeed, in 2020, each G7 country saw an increase in the percentage of the population reporting that they would feel very comfortable with a woman being the head of government or CEO of a major company in their country compared with 2019 (Kantar, 2020[99]).

References

Akerlof, G. and R. Kranton (2000), "Economics and Identity", *The Quarterly Journal of Economics*, Vol. 115/3, pp. 715-753, https://doi.org/10.1162/003355300554881. [48]

Atkinson, M., T. Greenstein and M. Lang (2005), "For Women, Breadwinning Can Be Dangerous: Gendered Resource Theory and Wife Abuse", *Journal of Marriage and Family*, Vol. 67/5, pp. 1137-1148, http://dx.doi.org/10.1111/j.1741-3737.2005.00206.x. [58]

Barker, G. et al. (2011), *Evolving Men: Initial Results from the International Men and Gender Equality Survey (IMAGES)*, Instituto Promundo, Rio de Janeiro and International Center for Research on Women (ICRW), Washington, D.C., https://www.icrw.org/wp-content/uploads/2016/10/Evolving-Men-Initial-Results-from-the-International-Men-and-Gender-Equality-Survey-IMAGES-1.pdf. [53]

Barker, G. et al. (2010), *What Men Have to Do With It: Public Policies to Promote Gender Equality*, ICRW, New Delhi and Promundo, Washington D.C., https://promundoglobal.org/wp-content/uploads/2014/12/What-Men-Have-to-Do-With-It.pdf. [52]

Barron, L. (2003), "Ask and you shall Receive? Gender Differences in Negotiators' Beliefs about Requests for a Higher Salary", *Human Relations*, Vol. 56/6, pp. 635-662, https://doi.org/10.1177/00187267030566001. [43]

Berdahl, J. (2007), "Harassment based on sex: Protecting social status in the context of gender hierarchy", *Academy of Management Review*, Vol. 32, pp. 641–658, http://dx.doi.org/10.2307/20159319. [55]

Berdahl, J. et al. (2018), "Work as a Masculinity Contest", *Journal of Social Issues*, Vol. 74/3, pp. 422-448, http://doi.wiley.com/10.1111/josi.12289. [6]

Bernard, J. (1993), *"The Good-Provider Role: Its rise and fall"*, HarperCollins, New York. [39]

Bertrand, M., E. Kamenica and J. Pan (2015), "Gender Identity and Relative Income within Households", *The Quarterly Journal of Economics*, Vol. 130/2, pp. 571-614, https://doi.org/10.1093/qje/qjv001. [7]

Bhalotra, S., R. Brulé and S. Roy (2017), *Women's Inheritance Rights Reform and the Preference for Sons in India*, IZA Institute of Labor Economics, http://ftp.iza.org/dp11239.pdf. [25]

Bhattacharya, H. (2015), "Spousal Violence and Women's Employment in India", *Feminist Economics*, Vol. 21/2, pp. 30-52, http://dx.doi.org/10.1080/13545701.2014.994653. [59]

Bolzendahl, C. and D. Myers (2004), "Feminist Attitudes and Support for Gender Equality: Opinion Change in Women and Men, 1974-1998", *Social Forces*, Vol. 83/2, pp. 759-789, http://dx.doi.org/10.1353/sof.2005.0005. [33]

Booysen, L. and S. Nkomo (2007), *New developments in employment equity and diversity management in South Africa*, Edward Elgar Publishing, http://dx.doi.org/10.4337/9780857939319.00018. [88]

Bosson, J. et al. (2009), "Precarious Manhood and Displays of Physical Aggression", *Personality and Social Psychology Bulletin*, Vol. 35/5, pp. 623-634, http://dx.doi.org/10.1177/0146167208331161. [56]

Botticini, M. and A. Siow (2003), "Why Dowries?", *American Economic Review*, Vol. 93/4, pp. 1385-1398, http://dx.doi.org/10.1257/000282803769206368. [26]

Brewster, K. and I. Padavic (2000), "Change in Gender-Ideology, 1977-1996:The Contributions of Intracohort Change and Population Turnover", *Journal of Marriage and Family*, Vol. 62/2, pp. 477-487, http://dx.doi.org/10.1111/j.1741-3737.2000.00477.x. [34]

Browning, M. and P. Chiappori (1998), "Efficient Intra-Household Allocations: A General Characterization and Empirical Tests", *Econometrica*, Vol. 66/6, pp. 1241–1278, http://www.jstor.org/stable/2999616. [50]

Buscatto, M. and B. Fusulier (2014), ""Masculinities" Challenged in Light of "Feminine" Occupations", *Recherches sociologiques et anthropologiques*, Vol. 44/2, pp. 1-19, https://doi.org/10.4000/rsa.1026. [62]

Caridad Bueno, C. and E. Henderson (2017), "Bargaining or Backlash? Evidence on Intimate Partner Violence from the Dominican Republic", *Feminist Economics*, Vol. 23/4, pp. 90-116, http://dx.doi.org/10.1080/13545701.2017.1292360. [60]

Connell, R. (1987), *Gender and Power: Society, the Person, and Sexual Politics*, Stanford University Press, Redwood City. [3]

Connell, R. et al. (1982), *Making the Difference: Schools, families and social division*, Allen & Unwin, Crows Nest. [82]

Cross, S. and B. Bagilhole (2002), "Girls' jobs for the boys? Men, masculinity and non-traditional occupations", *Gender, Work and Organization*, Vol. 9/2, pp. 204-226, http://onlinelibrary.wiley.com/doi/full/10.1111/1468-0432.00156. [67]

Dahl, J., T. Vescio and K. Weaver (2015), "How Threats to Masculinity Sequentially Cause Public Discomfort, Anger, and Ideological Dominance Over Women", *Social Psychology*, Vol. 46/4, pp. 242-254, https://doi.org/10.1027/1864-9335/a000248. [68]

Diekman, A. and A. Eagly (2000), "Stereotypes as Dynamic Constructs: Women and Men of the Past, Present, and Future", *Personality and Social Psychology Bulletin*, Vol. 26/10, pp. 1171-1188, http://dx.doi.org/10.1177/0146167200262001. [69]

Donnelly, K. et al. (2015), "Attitudes Toward Women's Work and Family Roles in the United States, 1976–2013", *Psychology of Women Quarterly*, Vol. 40/1, pp. 41-54, http://dx.doi.org/10.1177/0361684315590774. [36]

Eagly, C. (2004), *Women and men as leaders*, SAGE, Thousand Oaks. [84]

Eurobarometer (2017), *Special Eurobarometer 465: Gender Equality 2017*, EU Directorate-General for Communication, http://data.europa.eu/euodp/en/data/dataset/S2154_87_4_465_ENG. [17]

Ezzell, M. (2016), *Healthy for whom? Males, men, and masculinity: A reflection on the doing (and study) of dominance*, Oxford University Press, New York. [4]

Finnoff, K. (2012), "Intimate partner violence, female employment, and male backlash in Rwanda", *The economics of peace and security journal*, Vol. 7/2, https://www.epsjournal.org.uk/index.php/EPSJ/article/view/139/0. [61]

Fiske, S. and J. Berdahl (2007), *Social Power*, Guilford Publications, New York, https://www.guilford.com/excerpts/kruglanski.pdf?t. [71]

Focus 2030 and Women Deliver (2021), *Citizens Call for a Gender-Equal World. A Roadmap for Action: Findings from a 17-Country Public Opinion Survey on Gender Equality Prepared for the Generation Equality Forum*, https://womendeliver.org/wp-content/uploads/2021/02/Global_Report_English.pdf. [24]

Foster, A. and M. Rosenzweig (1999), *Missing Women, the Marriage Market and Economic Growth*, Stanford Center for International Development, https://kingcenter.stanford.edu/sites/default/files/publications/49wp_0.pdf. [23]

Gallup (2017), *Towards a better future for women and work:*, Gallup Analytics, https://www.ilo.org/wcmsp5/groups/public/---dgreports/---dcomm/---publ/documents/publication/wcms_546256.pdf. [37]

Gill, A. and T. Mitra-Kahn (2009), "Explaining Daughter Devaluation and the Issue of Missing Women in South Asia and the UK", *Current Sociology*, doi: 10.1177/0011392109337652, pp. 684-703, https://doi.org/10.1177/0011392109337652. [21]

Girlguiding (2018), *Girls' Attitudes Survey 2018*, Girlguiding, https://www.girlguiding.org.uk/globalassets/docs-and-resources/research-and-campaigns/girls-attitudes-survey-2018.pdf. [93]

Goode, W. (1994), *Why Men Resist*, HarperCollins, New York. [40]

Haerpfer, C. et al. (eds.) (2020), *World Values Survey: Round Seven – Country-Pooled Datafile*, JD Systems Institute & WVSA Secretariat, http://www.worldvaluessurvey.org/WVSDocumentationWV7.jsp (accessed on 18 August 2020). [15]

Halász, V. and R. Cunnington (2012), "Unconscious Effects of Action on Perception", *Brain Sciences*, Vol. 2/2, pp. 130-146, http://dx.doi.org/10.3390/brainsci2020130. [97]

Halvorsen, P. and J. Ljunggren (2020), "A new generation of business masculinity? Privileged high school boys in a gender egalitarian context", *Gender and Education*, pp. 1-15, http://www.tandfonline.com/action/journalInformation?journalCode=cgee20. [83]

Heilman, M. (2012), "Gender stereotypes and workplace bias", *Research in Organizational Behavior*, Vol. 32, pp. 113-135, http://dx.doi.org/10.1016/j.riob.2012.11.003. [78]

Heppner, R. (2013), *The Ideal Worker*, Palgrave Macmillan, New York, http://link.springer.com/chapter/10.1057/9781137350701_9. [75]

Holmes, J. (2006), *Gendered Talk at Work: Constructing Gender Identity through Workplace Discourse*, Blackwell, Oxford. [80]

Hryniewicz, L. and M. Vianna (2018), "Mulheres em posição de liderança: obstáculos e expectativas de gênero em cargos gerenciais", *Cadernos EBAPE.BR*, Vol. 16/3, pp. 331-344, http://dx.doi.org/10.1590/1679-395174876. [92]

Ibarra, H. and O. Obodaru (2009), *Women and the Vision Thing*, https://hbr.org/2009/01/women-and-the-vision-thing. [86]

ILO (2020), *Leading to Success: The business case for women in business management in Indonesia*, ILO, Geneva, https://www.ilo.org/wcmsp5/groups/public/---asia/---ro-bangkok/---ilo-jakarta/documents/publication/wcms_750802.pdf. [47]

ILO (2019), *SDG Indicator 5.2.2 - Female share of employment in managerial positions (%) - Annual*, https://www.ilo.org/shinyapps/bulkexplorer24/?lang=en&segment=indicator&id=SDG_0552_O CU_RT_A (accessed on 13 October 2020). [46]

ILO (2019), *The business case for change*, ILO, Geneva, https://www.ilo.org/wcmsp5/groups/public/---dgreports/---dcomm/---publ/documents/publication/wcms_700953.pdf. [45]

ILO (2018), *Global Wage Report 2018/19: What lies behind gender pay gaps*, ILO, Geneva, https://www.ilo.org/global/publications/books/WCMS_650553/lang--en/index.htm. [41]

ILO (2018), *World Employment and Social Outlook: Trends for Women 2018 – Global snapshot*, ILO, Geneva, https://www.ilo.org/global/research/global-reports/weso/trends-for-women2018/WCMS_619577/lang--en/index.htm. [31]

ILOSTAT (2020), *Labour statistics on women*, https://ilostat.ilo.org/topics/women/ (accessed on 13 October 2020). [20]

ILOStat (2021), *Statistics on the working-age population and labour force*, https://ilostat.ilo.org/topics/population-and-labour-force/. [18]

Ipsos (2019), *International Women's Day 2019: Global Attitudes towards Gender Equality*, https://www.ipsos.com/sites/default/files/ct/news/documents/2019-03/international-womens-day-2019-global-attitudes-towards-gender-equality.pdf. [89]

Ipsos (2019), *Perceptions of Masculinity & The Challenges of Opening Up*, https://cdn.movember.com/uploads/images/2012/News/UK%20IRE%20ZA/Movember%20Masculinity%20%26%20Opening%20Up%20Report%2008.10.19%20FINAL.pdf. [72]

IPU Parline (2020), *Monthly ranking of women in national parliaments*, https://data.ipu.org/women-ranking?month=7&year=2020 (accessed on 2 September 2020). [1]

Jayachandran, S. and I. Kuziemko (2011), "Why Do Mothers Breastfeed Girls Less than Boys? Evidence and Implications for Child Health in India", *The Quarterly Journal of Economics*, Vol. 126/3, pp. 1485-1538, http://dx.doi.org/10.1093/qje/qjr029. [27]

Kantar (2020), *The Reykjavik Index for Leadership 2020/21*, https://www.kantar.com/campaigns/reykjavik-index (accessed on 3 December 2020). [99]

Levant, R. et al. (2010), "Evaluation of the factor structure and construct validity of scores on the Male Role Norms Inventory—Revised (MRNI-R): Correction to Levant et al. 2010.", *Psychology of Men & Masculinity*, Vol. 11/3, pp. 181-181, https://doi.org/10.1037/a0019680. [74]

Lundberg, S. and R. Pollak (2008), *Family Decision-Making*, Palgrave Macmillan, London, https://doi.org/10.1057/978-1-349-95121-5_2551-1. [51]

Mahalik, J. et al. (2003), "Development of the Conformity to Masculine Norms Inventory", *Psychology of Men & Masculinity*, Vol. 4/1, pp. 3-25, http://www.psychwiki.com/dms/other/labgroup/Measu235sdgse5234234resWeek2/Krisztina2/Mahalik2003.pdf. [73]

McCormick-Huhn, K., L. Kim and S. Shields (2019), "Unconscious Bias Interventions for Business: An Initial Test of WAGES-Business (Workshop Activity for Gender Equity Simulation) and Google's "re:Work" Trainings", *Analyses of Social Issues and Public Policy*, http://dx.doi.org/10.1111/asap.12191. [94]

McKinsey & Co (2016), *Women Matter Africa*, https://www.mckinsey.com/featured-insights/gender-equality/women-matter-africa#. [2]

McLaughlin, H., C. Uggen and A. Blackstone (2012), "Sexual Harassment, Workplace Authority, and the Paradox of Power", *American Sociological Review*, Vol. 77/4, pp. 625-647, http://dx.doi.org/10.1177/0003122412451728. [57]

Mehta, C. and Y. Dementieva (2017), "The Contextual Specificity of Gender: Femininity and Masculinity in College Students' Same- and Other-Gender Peer Contexts", *Sex Roles*, Vol. 76/9-10, pp. 604-614, https://link.springer.com/article/10.1007%2Fs11199-016-0632-z. [11]

Miller, B. (1981), *The Endangered Sex: Neglect of Female Children in Rural North India*, Cornell University Press, Ithaca. [29]

Morgan, D. (1992), *Discovering Men: Critical Studies on Men and Masculinities*, Routledge, London. [70]

Moss-Racusin, C. et al. (2012), "Science faculty's subtle gender biases favor male students", *Proceedings of the National Academy of Sciences*, Vol. 109/41, pp. 16474-16479, http://dx.doi.org/10.1073/pnas.1211286109. [96]

Nanda, P. et al. (2014), *Study on Masculinity, Intimate Partner Violence and Son Preference in India*, International Center for Research on Women, New Delhi, https://www.icrw.org/wp-content/uploads/2016/10/Masculinity-Book_Inside_final_6th-Nov.pdf. [22]

Oakley, J. (2000), "Gender-based barriers to senior management positions: understanding the scarcity of female CEOs", *Journal of Business Ethics*, Vol. 27/4, pp. 321-334, http://dx.doi.org/10.1023/a:1006226129868. [90]

OECD (2020), "COVID-19 crisis in the MENA region: impact on gender equality and policy responses", *OECD Policy Responses to Coronavirus (COVID-19)*, https://www.oecd.org/coronavirus/policy-responses/covid-19-crisis-in-the-mena-region-impact-on-gender-equality-and-policy-responses-ee4cd4f4/#section-d1e240. [19]

OECD (2020), *Tackling discriminatory social institutions to pave the way towards women's full inclusion and gender equality in G20 countries*, OECD Development Centre, Paris, http://www.oecd.org/development/gender-development/W20_OECD_Final_Report.pdf. [42]

OECD (2019), *PISA 2018 Results (Volume II): Where All Students Can Succeed*, PISA, OECD Publishing, Paris, https://doi.org/10.1787/b5fd1b8f-en. [63]

OECD (2019), *SIGI 2019 Global Report: Transforming Challenges into Opportunities*, Social Institutions and Gender Index, OECD Publishing, Paris, https://dx.doi.org/10.1787/bc56d212-en. [9]

OECD (2018), *Burkin Faso Etude Pays SIGI*, OECD Development Centre, Paris, http://www.oecd.org/development/development-gender/ETUDE-PAYS-SIGI-BURKINA-FASO.pdf. [14]

OECD (2016), *OECD Employment Database*, https://stats.oecd.org/index.aspx?queryid=54760. [77]

OECD (2016), *Walking the tightrope: Background brief on parents' work-life balance across the stages of childhood*, OECD Publishing, Paris, http://www.oecd.org/social/family/Background-brief-parents-work-life-balance-stages-childhood.pdf. [32]

OECD (2015), *The ABC of Gender Equality in Education: Aptitude, Behaviour, Confidence*, PISA, OECD Publishing, Paris, http://dx.doi.org/10.1787/9789264229945-en. [64]

Oster, E. (2009), "Proximate Sources of Population Sex Imbalance in India", *Demography*, Vol. 46/2, pp. 325-339, http://dx.doi.org/10.1353/dem.0.0055. [28]

Parker, K. and R. Stepler (2017), *Americans see men as the financial providers, even as women's contributions grow*, https://www.pewresearch.org/fact-tank/2017/09/20/americans-see-men-as-the-financial-providers-even-as-womens-contributions-grow/. [16]

Pew Research Center (2015), *Women and Leadership*, https://www.pewsocialtrends.org/2015/01/14/women-and-leadership/. [91]

Poynting, S. and M. Donaldson (2005), "Snakes and Leaders", *Men and Masculinities*, Vol. 7/4, pp. 325-346, http://dx.doi.org/10.1177/1097184x03260968. [81]

Raley, S., M. Mattingly and S. Bianchi (2006), "How Dual Are Dual-Income Couples? Documenting Change From 1970 to 2001", *Journal of Marriage and Family*, Vol. 68/1, pp. 11-28, http://dx.doi.org/10.1111/j.1741-3737.2006.00230.x. [38]

Schein, V. (2007), "Women in management: reflections and projections", *Women in Management Review*, Vol. 22/1, pp. 6-18, http://dx.doi.org/10.1108/09649420710726193. [87]

Schein, V. et al. (1996), "Think manager—think male: a global phenomenon?", *Journal of Organizational Behavior*, Vol. 17/1, https://doi.org/10.1002/(SICI)1099-1379(199601)17:1%3C33::AID-JOB778%3E3.0.CO;2-F.
[85]

Schrock, D. and M. Schwalbe (2009), "Men, Masculinity, and Manhood Acts", *Annual Review of Sociology*, Vol. 35/1, pp. 277-295, http://www.annualreviews.org/doi/10.1146/annurev-soc-070308-115933.
[5]

Sen, A. (1990), "More Than 100 Million Women Are Missing", *New York Review of Books*, Vol. 37/20, https://web.archive.org/web/20130504072819/http:/ucatlas.ucsc.edu/gender/Sen100M.html.
[30]

Silberschmidt, M. (2001), "Disempowerment of Men in Rural and Urban East Africa: Implications for Male Identity and Sexual Behavior", *World Development*, Vol. 29/4, pp. 657-671, http://dx.doi.org/10.1016/s0305-750x(00)00122-4.
[54]

Simpson, R. (2004), "Masculinity at Work: The Experiences of Men in Female Dominated Occupations", *Work, Employment and Society*, doi: 10.1177/09500172004042773, pp. 349-368, http://doi.org/10.1177/09500172004042773.
[8]

UN Women (2019), *He For She: 2019 Impact Report*, UN, Geneva, https://www.heforshe.org/sites/default/files/2019-09/HeForShe%202019%20IMPACT%20Report_Full.pdf.
[10]

UNESCO (2018), *Global education monitoring report gender review 2018: Meeting our commitments to gender equality in education*, UN, Geneva, https://unesdoc.unesco.org/ark:/48223/pf0000261593.
[44]

UNESCO (2017), *Cracking the code: girls' and women's education in science, technology, engineering and mathematics (STEM)*, https://unesdoc.unesco.org/ark:/48223/pf0000253479.
[65]

UNFPA Ukraine (2018), *Masculinity today: Men's attitudes towards gender stereotypes and violence against women*, UNFPA, Kyiv, https://promundoglobal.org/wp-content/uploads/2018/06/Masculinity-Today-Mens_Report.pdf.
[49]

UNFPA/SCFWCA (2018), *Gender equality and gender relations in Azerbaijan: current trends and opportunities. Findings from the Men and Gender Equality Survey (IMAGES)*, UNFPA Azerbaijan, Baku, https://promundoglobal.org/wp-content/uploads/2018/12/IMAGES-Azerbaijan-report.pdf.
[13]

Waismel-Manor, R., A. Levanon and P. Tolbert (2016), "The impact of family economic structure on dual-earners' career and family satisfaction", http://digitalcommons.ilr.cornell.edu/articles/1072.
[35]

Williams, C. (ed.) (1993), *Doing "Women's Work": Men in Nontraditional Occupations*, SAGE Publishing Inc., Newbury Park.
[66]

Williams, J. (2001), *Unbending Gender: Why Family and Work Conflict and What To Do About It*, Oxford University Press, Oxford.
[79]

Williams, J., M. Blair-Loy and J. Berdahl (2013), "Cultural Schemas, Social Class, and the Flexibility Stigma", *Journal of Social Issues*, Vol. 69/2, pp. 209-234, http://dx.doi.org/10.1111/josi.12012.
[76]

Williams, M. (2005), *Leadership for leaders*, Thorogood, London. [98]

Wynn, A. and S. Correll (2018), "Puncturing the pipeline: Do technology companies alienate women in recruiting sessions?", *Social Studies of Science*, Vol. 48/1, pp. 149-164, http://dx.doi.org/10.1177/0306312718756766. [95]

Zuo, J. and S. Tang (2000), "Breadwinner status and gender ideologies of men and women regarding family roles", *Sociological Perspectives*, Vol. 43/1, pp. 29-43, http://www.jstor.org/stable/1389781. [12]

Notes

[1] For a list of countries/territories included in all surveys referenced in this publication, please see the Annex.

[2] The term "missing women" indicates a shortfall in the number of women relative to the expected number of women in a region or country.

[3] Vertical segregation describes men's domination of the highest status jobs in both traditionally masculine and traditionally feminine occupations, while horizontal segregation refers to differences in the number of people of each gender present across occupations (see Chapter 2, Section 3).

[4] The variation of the gender pay gap between managers and all employees may reflect various issues, including occupational segregation in the labour market and management position; the overall proportion of women in management positions compared with their labour force participation; the structure of the economy in terms of industries and occupations where men and women are concentrated; gender-equitable government policies and their implementation; and social norms.

[5] All countries provide women with the same rights as men to hold public and political office in the legislature and all countries except Oman provide women with the same rights as men to hold public and political office in the executive branch.

3 Masculinities and women's empowerment in the private sphere

This chapter presents five norms of restrictive masculinities that directly affect women's and girls' empowerment and well-being in the private sphere. These norms dictate that a "real" man should: i) not do unpaid care and domestic work, ii) have the final say in household decisions, iii) control household assets, iv) protect and exercise guardianship of women in the household, and v) dominate sexual and reproductive choices. Each of these norms reinforces the discriminatory social institutions that govern the private sphere, revealing one of the reasons why change in this area has been so slow. Nevertheless, gender-equitable masculinities are also emerging in the private sphere, evidence of which is highlighted in this chapter.

Introduction

While the private sphere has traditionally been seen as the domain of women, men continue to control, dominate and exercise power with regard to household decisions and practices. Social expectations of men in the private sphere encompass critical areas such as household decision making generally, and specific choices regarding the actions of family members, household assets, family planning and the household division of labour. This chapter discusses five norms of restrictive masculinities in the private sphere which dictate that a "real" man should: i) not do unpaid care and domestic work, ii) have the final say in household decisions, iii) control household assets, iv) protect and exercise guardianship of women in the household, and v) dominate sexual and reproductive choices (Figure 3.1). These five norms reveal the important role that restrictive masculinities play in the private sphere and their related consequences for women's empowerment and gender equality. While not all households are composed of different-sex partners, and restrictive masculinities can directly harm lesbian, gay, bisexual, transgender and intersex (LGBTI) people (Box 3.1), much of the data that is widely available concerning gender dynamics in the private sphere is oriented towards heterosexual couples and the consequences faced by women that result from these unequal gender dynamics within the household. As such, this chapter mainly focuses on different-sex couples and the consequences faced by women in these partnerships.

Figure 3.1. Defining norms of restrictive masculinities in the private sphere

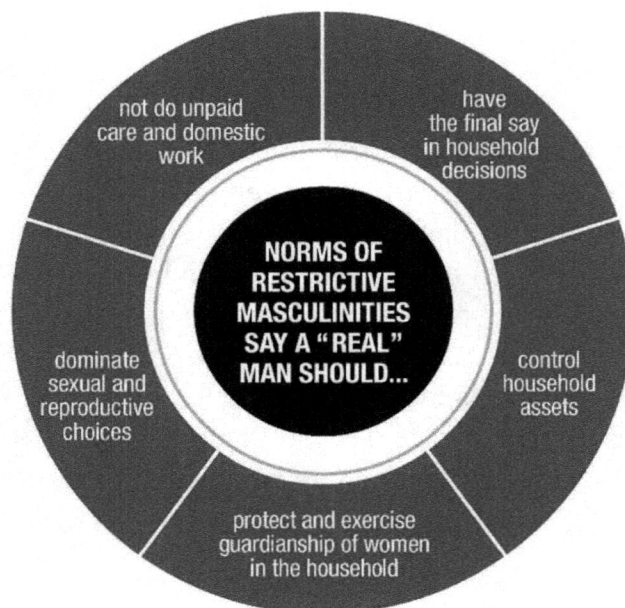

Source: Authors' elaboration.

Box 3.1. Addressing restrictive masculinities can also promote LGBTI inclusion

Wide acceptance of restrictive masculinities confines men and boys to rigid scripts of manhood which can directly harm LGBTI people and their inclusion in societies. Restrictive masculinities are based on a rigid understanding of the gender binary, leaving little room for the recognition and inclusion of non-binary, trans and intersex individuals. This upholds discriminatory practices on the basis of gender identity and intersex status that negatively affect the well-being of these individuals in diverse areas including in terms of education, health, family life and economic outcomes (Valfort, 2017[1]). Indeed, data show that less than one-half (44%) of respondents in 17 Organisation for Economic Co-operation and Development (OECD) member countries would accept a transgender child (OECD, 2019[2]).

Moreover, rigid heterosexuality and homophobia are also features of restrictive masculinities (Heilman, Barker and Harrison, 2017[3]). The expectation that "real" men are heterosexual is linked to homophobia as restrictive understandings of manhood view homosexuality as an affront to masculinity. This view has severe consequences for lesbian, gay and bisexual people specifically as it upholds widespread homophobia, which is often accompanied by violence against LGBTI people.

Efforts to shift restrictive masculinities towards gender-equitable alternatives can promote gender equality, which is strongly correlated with LGBTI inclusion. Research shows that gender equality is positively correlated with the inclusion of LGBTI people in legal frameworks through specific protections against discrimination (OECD, 2020[4]).

Exploring restrictive masculinities in the private sphere is key to understanding why discriminatory social norms in the household are so resistant to change. Despite the fact that issues within the private sphere – such as unpaid care and domestic work, intimate partner violence and household decision making – have attracted more attention from the media, researchers and policy makers, social norms and practices in these spaces have changed either slowly or not at all (OECD, 2019[5]). This has important consequences for women and girls, as lacking agency and decision-making power regarding their time, bodies and resources directly hinders their empowerment. Moreover, in the private sphere, norms of restrictive masculinities can give rise to physical, sexual, psychological and economic violence which can further entrench male dominance. An understanding of the restrictive masculinities in this area gives a clearer picture of the deeply entrenched social norms that hinder women's empowerment as well as the pathways to transform masculinities, and in turn, the lives of women and men. In this regard, public policies and programmes are pivotal. The notions and ideals about how men should or are expected to behave, held by both communities and individuals, are shaped, at least in part, by states' policies and equality discourses which can foster supportive environments and create incentives for societies to adopt more gender-equitable ideals of masculinity (Segal, 1993[6]).

Masculinities have an important role to play in facilitating women's empowerment in the private sphere, the pursuit of which can give way to new, gender-equitable masculinities. In the private sphere, gender-equitable masculinities emphasise open communication and collaboration, leading to joint decision making on household matters. Where these norms are widely accepted, societies encourage women to be autonomous decision makers over their own bodies and freedom of movement. In promoting more gender-equal divisions of household labour, these new masculinities do not define men's role in the household as strictly providers. Rather, they allow for men's fuller engagement in all aspects of household life, especially including caring. With regard to fatherhood, evidence has shown that becoming a parent can be a moment in which men exhibit "caring masculinities" (Elliott, 2015[7]). In a gender-equal world, societies may come to expect this from fathers, and states will provide the necessary institutional frameworks for men to be caring and active parents. This positive vision requires that understandings of what it means to be a "real" man in the private sphere move beyond the "scripts" provided by restrictive masculinities.

This chapter is structured around five defining features of restrictive masculinities in the private sphere. For each of these defining features, this chapter investigates their consequences for women's empowerment and provides evidence of gender-equitable alternatives.

1. Norms of restrictive masculinities dictate that a "real" man should not do unpaid care and domestic work

Norms of restrictive masculinities uphold unpaid care and domestic work as the domain of women and stigmatise men's active participation (Greene, Robles and Pawlak, 2011[8]). Not only do femininities play a role in women's involvement in unpaid care work, but masculinities, particularly restrictive masculinities, uphold unequal divisions of household labour. Women can affirm their feminine identity through care and housework, whereas men can affirm their masculine identity through avoiding this work (Bittman et al., 2003[9]; Thébaud, 2010[10]). In the United States and Mexico, for example, in 2017, 46% and 41% of men, respectively, reported that society tells them that "a husband should not have to do household chores" (Heilman, Barker and Harrison, 2017[3]). Also in 2017, in Burkina Faso, 81% of respondents declared that childcare and domestic work is women's prerogative, and 28% of female respondents and 40% of male respondents thought that a man who stays at home to take care of his children and the home is less of a man (OECD, 2018[11]). Similarly, 69% of respondents disagreed with the idea that unpaid care and housework should be equally distributed between women and men when both have paid employment outside the home (OECD, 2018[11]).

While women have taken on more paid labour since the start of the 20th century, men's contribution to unpaid care and domestic work has not increased enough to compensate for this change (Latshaw and Hale, 2016[12]; Thébaud, 2010[10]). In fact, evidence shows that men in heterosexual relationships whose partner earns more than them may actually take on less of this work (Bittman et al., 2003[9]; Latshaw and Hale, 2016[12]; Sevilla-Sanz, Gimenez-Nadal and Fernández, 2010[13]; Thébaud, 2010[10]) (see Chapter 2, Section 2). This has been interpreted as a way for men to reaffirm their masculinity and to compensate for deviating from traditional gender norms, and thus allowing them to maintain their "authority with minimal responsibility" (Bittman et al., 2003[9]; Thébaud, 2010[10]; Uchendu, 2009[14]). This suggests that the division of labour within the household is not perfectly linked to unequal bargaining power or one-to-one exchanges – as assumed by the family economic literature – and that gender norms play a significant role (Browning and Chiappori, 1998[15]; Thébaud, 2010[10]). The fact that care, and the domestic sphere in general, is understood to be feminine constitutes a critical barrier to the valuation of this work and men's greater engagement in unpaid care and domestic work (Hanlon, 2012[16]). Indeed, in 2020, 8% of respondents in Colombia and 42% of respondents in India reported that it is acceptable "to let women do the majority of housework, childcare and elderly care" (Focus 2030 and Women Deliver, 2021[17]). Similarly, in 2017, 15% and 16% of respondents in the Czech Republic and Lithuania, respectively, disapproved of a man doing an equal share of household activities as a woman (Eurobarometer, 2017[18]).

Legal frameworks uphold the expectation that unpaid care work is feminine, and thus it is not "men's work". In 2019, 60 countries[1] had legal frameworks that did not provide women with the same rights as men to be the guardians of their children (OECD, 2019[5]). Furthermore, only 39 countries mandate paid paternity leave, compared with 173 countries which mandate paid maternity leave (OECD, 2019[5]). While paternity leave entitlements are a relatively recent phenomenon – among all Organisation for Economic Co-operation and Development (OECD) countries, only three[2] had legislated paternity leave in 1970 – progress in legal reform has been slow (OECD, 2020[19]). The persistent discrepancies between leave for mothers and fathers send a clear signal that societies believe caring for children is predominately a task for women and that they condone restrictive masculinities' vision of detached fatherhood. Moreover, even when policies are in place that allow men an allotment of leave, the entitlements are short and the majority of men do not take full advantage of them. For example, in 2009-10, 31% of working men in India took no leave after the birth of their most recent child, whereas 77% of Chilean men and 60% of Croatian men reported the same (Barker et al., 2011[20]). Furthermore, as society expects men to prioritise their career over their private life, fathers benefitting from paternity and/or parental leaves may face stigmatisation (Dahl, Løken and Mogstad, 2014[21]) (see Chapter 2, Section 4). In the 27 countries for which data are available, on average, 18% of respondents declared in 2019 that a man who stays home to look after his children is less of a man, and this was as high as 76% in Korea (Ipsos, 2019[22]) (Figure 3.2).

While paternity leave uptake remains low, there is significant support for policies to allow men to better balance work and family life. For example, in 2019, more than 58% of people across all 27 surveyed countries reported agreeing or strongly agreeing that "employers should make it easier for men to combine childcare with work" (Ipsos, 2019[22]). Moreover, evidence from Nordic countries shows that father-friendly initiatives, together with widespread acceptance of men's involvement in caring practices, can lead more men to take paternity leave (Lund, Meriläinen and Tienari, 2019[23]). Indeed, in 2013, for every 100 children born in Sweden and Finland, more than 70 and 80 individuals, respectively, claimed publicly administered paternity benefits or publicly administered paternity leave (OECD, 2016[24]). Further evidence shows that taking paternity leave can have a lasting impact on fathers' engagement in unpaid care work and women's employment (Amin, Islam and Sakhonchik, 2016[25]; OECD, 2019[26]).

Figure 3.2. Unequal divisions of unpaid care work between men and women are related to norms of restrictive masculinities around care

Percentage of the population that agrees or strongly agrees that "A man who stays home to look after his children is less of a man" by the female to male ratio of time spent on unpaid, domestic and volunteer work in a 24-hour period

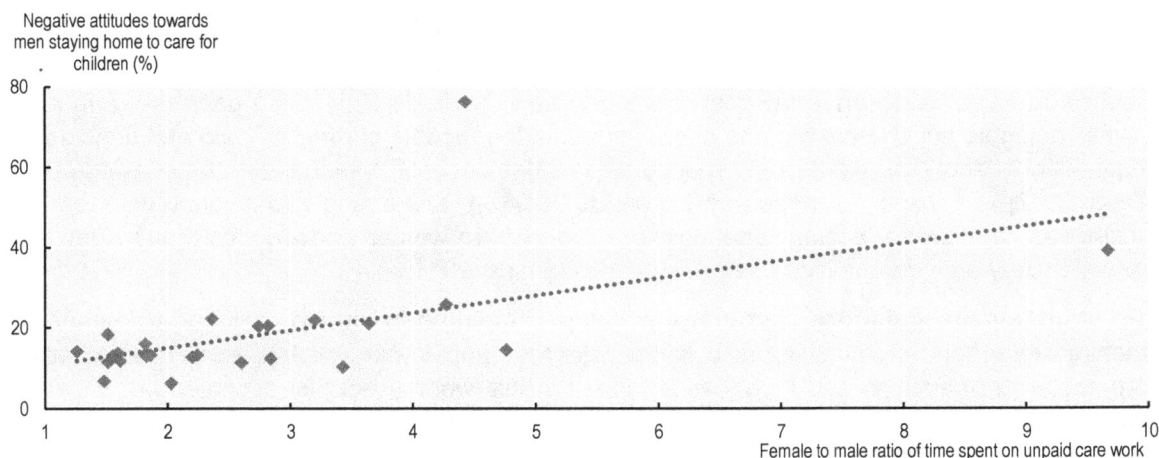

Note: Negative attitudes towards men staying home to care for children refers to the percentage of respondents agreeing with the statement "A man who stays home to look after his children is less of a man". R^2=0.3007.
Sources: (Ipsos, 2019[22]), "Global Attitudes Towards Gender Equality", https://www.ipsos.com/en/men-are-not-emasculated-caring-children-need-support-employers; and (OECD, 2019[27]), Gender Institutions and Development Database (GID-DB), https://stats.oecd.org/Index.aspx?DataSetCode=GIDDB2019.

StatLink ᐧᐧᔓ https://doi.org/10.1787/888934230471

Even when men do engage in unpaid care and domestic work, the division of tasks reveals gendered associations. There are numerous tasks within the category of domestic work, including cleaning, cooking, washing clothes and maintaining the home. "Women primarily do the tasks that traditionally have been thought of as 'women's work' (e.g. cooking, laundry, housecleaning), whereas men primarily do 'male' tasks (e.g. yard work, auto maintenance)" (Greenstein, 2000[28]). Across all four countries with available data, in 2017, more than 90% of women reported cleaning the bathroom and cooking in the previous month, whereas men's participation in these tasks varied (El Feki, Heilman and Barker, 2017[29]). For example, in 2017, between 6% of men in Egypt and 26% of men in Lebanon reported doing laundry in the previous month, but when it came to cooking, men appeared to be more engaged (El Feki, Heilman and Barker, 2017[29]). In the same year, between 27% of men in the Palestinian Authority and 64% of men in Lebanon reported that they had carried out this task in the previous month (El Feki, Heilman and Barker, 2017[29]). A common rule in the household division of tasks emerges from this kind of analysis: "the greater the social orientation of a task, the more feminine; the more technical orientation of the task, the more masculine" (Barker et al., 2011[20]).

When it comes to unpaid care-related tasks such as childcare, there are clear divisions as well. In 2017, the vast majority of fathers reported playing with their children several times or more per week; however, when it comes to changing diapers and cooking for their children, a significantly smaller percentage reported carrying out these care tasks (Barker et al., 2011[20]; El Feki, Heilman and Barker, 2017[29]). Social norms and practices such as this gendered task division sustain each other, and attitudinal data show that in the majority of countries with available data, more than 50% of men agree that "changing diapers, giving kids a bath and feeding kids are a mother's responsibility"[3] (Barker et al., 2011[20]; van der Gaag et al., 2019[30]).

Unpaid care work is essential to the functioning of society, and this work mostly falls on women's shoulders when men conform to norms of restrictive masculinities. Globally, women undertake 75% of unpaid care and domestic work (OECD, 2019[5]). In 2019, in terms of time, women globally averaged five hours of unpaid care work per day, compared with just two hours for men (OECD, 2019[5]). Each moment women spend on unpaid care work represents time that could have been spent on paid work, pursuing entrepreneurship, improving skills or pursuing education (Ferrant and Thim, 2016[31]; Ferrant, Pesando and Nowacka, 2014[32]). The time burdens of unpaid care work perpetuate women's lower rates of labour force participation and may push women to seek flexibility by working part time or in informal jobs. While doing so might allow them to better negotiate the "double burden" of paid and unpaid work, it also negatively affects their advancement opportunities, job security, remuneration and savings (Ferrant and Thim, 2016[31]; Ferrant, Pesando and Nowacka, 2014[32]). The struggle to balance work and home responsibilities can lead to "occupational downgrading", where women choose jobs that are low paying and for which they are overqualified (Hegewisch and Gornick, 2011[33]).

Gender-equitable masculinities encourage active participation in unpaid care and domestic work. In societies where gender-equitable masculinities take root, unpaid care work is recognised as essential to the functioning of society, and men's engagement in this work is not just accepted but is expected. Moreover, the distribution of this work shifts, with men taking on their fair share, thus allowing women more time to devote to their careers, well-being and interests. While targeted interventions which engage men and boys in unpaid care and domestic work have shown that attitudinal and behavioural change is possible (Barker, 2007[34]; Doyle et al., 2018[35]), large-scale redistribution of this unpaid work between men and women has yet to take place (OECD, 2019[5]). Nevertheless, there is great potential for policies to effect major change in this area and beyond, as "[t]here is a direct correspondence between sharing power in more public domains and sharing the care and drudgery of domestic life in the family domain" (Kimmel, Hearn and Connell, 2005[36]).

Unlike restrictive masculinities which emphasise fathers' roles as financial providers, gender-equitable masculinities promote expanded understandings of fatherhood and male involvement in caregiving (Johansson, 2011[37]; UNFPA/Promundo, 2018[38]). Becoming a father can mark a critical turning point in the lives of men, and also often involves changing habits and routines as well as navigating new social expectations (van der Gaag et al., 2019[30]). Where gender-equitable masculinities are more widely accepted, societies come to expect fathers to be actively engaged in caring for their children. Evidence from countries such as Australia, Denmark, Finland, Iceland, Indonesia, Spain, Sweden, the United Kingdom and the United States suggests that it is becoming more common for fathers to exhibit "caring masculinities and interchangeable parenting roles" (Cederström, 2019[39]; van der Gaag et al., 2019[30]). Indeed, on average, 85% of fathers across seven countries surveyed in the Helping Dads Care Research Project (2017-2019) reported agreeing with the statement: "I will do whatever it takes to be very involved in the early weeks and/or months of caring for my newly born or adopted child" (van der Gaag et al., 2019[30]).

2. Norms of restrictive masculinities dictate that a "real" man should have the final say in household decisions

Dominance in household decision making represents a way for men to exercise power over women and other members of the household. Decision making is an expression of power, not just in the form of individual agency but also "power over", which forms the very basis of gender inequalities (MenEngage, n.d.[40]). Being the main decision maker and having the final say in household decisions means having disproportionate influence on family affairs, relationships and the activities of other household members. Hence, dominating decisions in the household enables men to exert power and control in the private sphere and over other individuals.

Norms of restrictive masculinities include the expectation that men have the final say in household decisions. Being a "real" man notably implies being in control of decisions in the private sphere. More than 80% of respondents in Niger, the United Republic of Tanzania (hereafter "Tanzania") and Central Uganda reported that most people in their community expect men to have the final say regarding decisions in the home (Levtov et al., 2018[41]; Spindler et al., 2019[42]; Vlahovicova et al., 2019[43]). In 16 out of 25 countries for which data are available, at least two-thirds of men agreed that a man should have the final word about decisions in his home (van der Gaag et al., 2019[30]) (Figure 3.3).

Legal frameworks can reinforce men's role as the main decision maker in the household. In some countries, national legislation upholds men's control over the private sphere and encourages the continuation of restrictive masculinities. Indeed, in 40 countries, the law does not provide women with the same rights as men to be recognised as the head of household, thus sending a strong message about men's superiority over women in their households (OECD, 2019[5]).

The norm of restrictive masculinities associated with male dominance in household decision making can undermine women's agency and curtail their empowerment opportunities. If men adhere to these social expectations encouraging them to have the final say in household decisions, they enjoy greater decision-making power and influence over family affairs than other household members. Large proportions of men and women reported that men dominate decisions that affect other household members. Nearly one-third of study respondents in Tanzania and Ukraine and more than three-quarters of male respondents in Azerbaijan and Central Uganda believed that men have more say than women in important decisions that affect them (Levtov et al., 2018[41]; UNFPA Ukraine, 2018[44]; UNFPA/SCFWCA, 2018[45]; Vlahovicova et al., 2019[43]). In circumstances where men have the final say, the consideration of women's preferences depends on the approval of their husband, who may choose to override their concerns. If women's convictions and preferences carry less weight in decisions than their husbands' do, it is difficult for women to assert themselves in the household and pursue their own goals and ambitions. This has important implications for women's individual agency and for gender equality in society overall (Greene, Robles and Pawlak, 2011[8]).

Figure 3.3. A high percentage of men report that a man should have the final word on household decisions

Percentage of men agreeing with the statement: "a man should have the final word about decisions in his home"

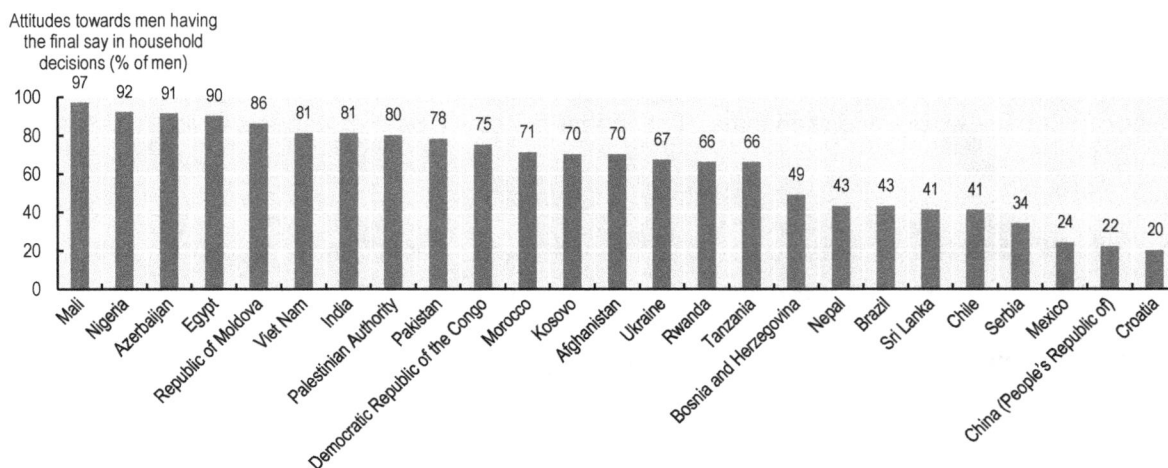

Note: Men believing that men should have the final say in household decisions refers to the percentage of men who report agreeing with the statement: "a man should have the final word about decisions in his home".
Source: (van der Gaag et al., 2019[30]), State of the World's Fathers: Unlocking the Power of Men's Care, https://men-care.org/wp-content/uploads/sites/3/2019/06/SOWF-2019_006_WEB.pdf; and (UNFPA/SCFWCA, 2018[45]), Gender equality and gender relations in Azerbaijan: current trends and opportunities. Findings from the Men and Gender Equality Survey (IMAGES), https://promundoglobal.org/wp-content/uploads/2018/12/IMAGES-Azerbaijan-report.pdf.

StatLink https://doi.org/10.1787/888934230490

Masculinities equated with male dominance and leadership in the household may also facilitate and legitimise the use of violence against women and children. Having the final say means having a veto in household decision making. This powerful position gives a man, as the head of the household, the capacity to define what can and cannot be done by other household members. Furthermore, violence may be used as a means to punish those who disregard a man's decisions, thus serving as a tool to preserve or re-establish male power when it has been challenged. Rigid social norms in the private sphere seem to condone the use of violence if women do not obey their husbands' decisions in various contexts (OECD, 2019[5]).

Unlike restrictive masculinities, gender-equitable masculinities do not expect men to be the head of the household or have the final say in household decisions. Gender-equitable norms promote joint household decision making and grant men and women equal decision-making power and freedom to choose for themselves. Gender-equitable masculinities do not operate in a framework which assigns fixed roles to men and women in the household. Characterised by flexibility, norms of gender-equitable masculinities encourage dynamics where men and women communicate with each other and overcome the gender binary. This means that both men and women influence family and relationship affairs without predefined power imbalances and the pressures of male dominance.

Social norms which encourage joint decision making seem to be evolving in various countries around the world. In Uganda and Zambia, for example, the proportion of women reporting that they alone or jointly have the final say in decisions regarding major household purchases, visits to family and friends, and healthcare increased from 32% (in 2000-01) to 58% and 67%, respectively, within about 15 years

(DHS, n.d.[46]). In Jordan, the share of women participating in these three decisions also increased by about 15 percentage points between 2007 and 2017 (DHS, n.d.[46]).

3. Norms of restrictive masculinities dictate that a "real" man should control household assets

Restrictive masculinities prescribe that a "real" man controls household assets and finances. Men's designated role as the financial provider constitutes a key component of restrictive masculinities. This primarily concerns the acquisition of money, but being the primary earner in a household is also a powerful position that underpins traditional notions of power and authority (Hunter, Riggs and Augoustinos, 2017[47]). Beyond earning money, men can solidify their authority by controlling and administering household assets. Dominating financial decision making is key to preserving control in the private sphere, as the manner in which household income is spent affects the well-being and opportunities of household members. This may be of particular importance as social norms and practices change with regard to women's labour force participation. With women contributing to the household income, men may find it hard to fulfil their expected role as financial providers (see Chapter 2, Section 1). In response, men may seek out ways to ensure their place as the head of the household – controlling household finances and resources can be one such way to preserve power in the home (Dolan, 2003[48]). This may concern decision-making authority over household expenditure, including spending on necessities such as food and clothing, as well as long-term financial investments, large purchases and savings.

Legal frameworks in some countries reinforce restrictive masculinities by strengthening men's authority over financial decision making and legally preventing women from having financial independence. While most countries allow women to open bank accounts in the same manner as men, four countries have legal frameworks that require married women to get permission from their husbands to open a bank account at a formal financial institution (OECD, 2019[5]). When it comes to decision making over land assets, the legal frameworks of 15 countries do not provide married women with the same rights as married men to own, administer and make decisions over land (OECD, 2019[5]). In 30 countries, this is also the case with regard to property and other non-land assets (OECD, 2019[5]).

If men adhere to the social expectation that they should control household assets and finances, women lack equal access to administer and use resources. In many countries, men continue to dominate decisions about household assets and finances (Bannon and Correia, 2006[49]; OECD, 2019[5]). In almost one-half of the countries for which data are available, at least one in three men and women reported that the husband/male partner is the main decision maker regarding large household purchases (DHS, n.d.[46]). In contrast, in only two of the countries for which data are available in the 2016-18 period, one in three respondents reported that the female partner is the main decision maker regarding large purchases (DHS, n.d.[46]). In Uganda, for example, women only make up one-third of owners or co-owners of land, and more than one-quarter of the population supports unequal rights to land for men and women (OECD, 2015[50]). Even in cases where women own assets, men have at least some control over their financial management. In Kenya and Tanzania, for example, less than one-half of women reported that they are able to sell their assets without consulting their husband (Njuki and Sanginga, 2013[51]). For women owners of dairy cattle and sheep in Kenya, fewer than one in ten reported that they can sell their livestock without consulting their husband while more than one in ten women reported that their husband has sole decision-making authority over the sale of the animals (Njuki and Sanginga, 2013[51]).

Furthermore, if women internalise these restrictive gender norms, they may defer financial decision making and underestimate their own ability to manage resources. A majority of female respondents reported deferring long-term financial decision making to their husband in Germany, Hong Kong (China), Singapore, Switzerland, the United Kingdom and the United States (UBS, 2019[52]).[4] Indeed, 82% reported doing so because they think their spouse knows more about this topic than they do, while 58% reported that their spouse never encouraged or invited them to be more involved (UBS, 2019[52]). These dynamics indicate that women are likely to be unaware of important decisions affecting the long-term well-being of their household and may lack the skills or confidence to take on a bigger role or manage their finances independently (Hung, Yoong and Brown, 2012[53]).

The control of men over household assets may have adverse effects on family well-being. Women's management of household assets is associated with positive development outcomes at the individual and household levels (Johnson et al., 2016[54]), and women are more likely to invest in children than men are, including children's education and clothing (Quisumbing and Maluccio, 2000[55]). Hence, assets controlled by women are more likely to positively affect the next generation (Quisumbing and Maluccio, 2000[55]). Furthermore, men tend to be less likely to allocate money towards daughters and may therefore risk neglecting their needs and aspirations (Nikiforidis et al., 2017[56]).

The social norm prescribing men's control over household finances also undermines efforts to improve women's empowerment. Increased access to empowerment opportunities for women does not automatically improve women's situation. If men control financial resources, women may fail to achieve economic independence despite the availability of new opportunities through empowerment programmes. Furthermore, improved access to financial resources has, in some cases, led to violent responses among men (Ahmed, 2008[57]). Men can feel threatened by increases in women's relative independence and resort to physical violence to re-establish their dominance and control in the household (Sanders, 2015[58]). Analysis of a microfinance programme in Bangladesh, for instance, showed that women's access to microcredit without the involvement of men can exacerbate intimate partner violence and prevent joint decision making regarding credit (Ahmed, 2008[57]). Similar evidence has been found for cash transfers that primarily target women (Manley and Slavchevska, 2016[59]). Involving men in economic empowerment interventions has, in contrast, been proven to avoid violent backlash and improve women's economic situation (Kim et al., 2009[60]).

Men's control over household finances can prevent women from leaving their partner in cases of intimate partner violence. If men control household finances, they have the power to prevent their female partner from accessing resources and administrating money. Interference with women's ability to manage and use economic resources is likely to impede their ability to achieve economic self-sufficiency (Postmus et al., 2020[61]). Women who are financially dependent on their husband are less likely to leave their partner in the case of physical and/or sexual violence (Anderson and Saunders, 2003[62]; Sanders, 2015[58]). Material resources, i.e. income and employment, are important predictors of women leaving abusive relationships (Anderson and Saunders, 2003[62]), and further evidence suggests that women who participate in financial decision making are less likely to experience intimate partner violence in the first place (Akilova and Marti, 2014[63]).

Gender-equitable masculinities are gaining prominence when it comes to financial decision making. These norms support women in accessing and managing financial resources according to their needs and preferences. For example, joint asset management has become increasingly common since the early 2000s (El Feki, Heilman and Barker, 2017[29]). Male respondents are less likely to hold sole decision-making authority over household finances than their fathers did during their childhood (El Feki, Heilman and Barker, 2017[29]). Furthermore, in 2016-18 women were more likely to report joint decision making with their husband on large household purchases than they were 15 years earlier in seven out of eight countries for which data are available (DHS, n.d.[46]) (Figure 3.4). Finally, between 2010 and 2018, 53-95% of female respondents reported that they alone or jointly have the final say in making daily purchases in countries for which data are available (DHS, n.d.[46]).

Figure 3.4. In most countries, more women reported being involved in decisions at home in 2016-18 than did so in 2001-03

Percentage of women who reported that the main decision maker regarding large purchases is the respondent and her husband jointly

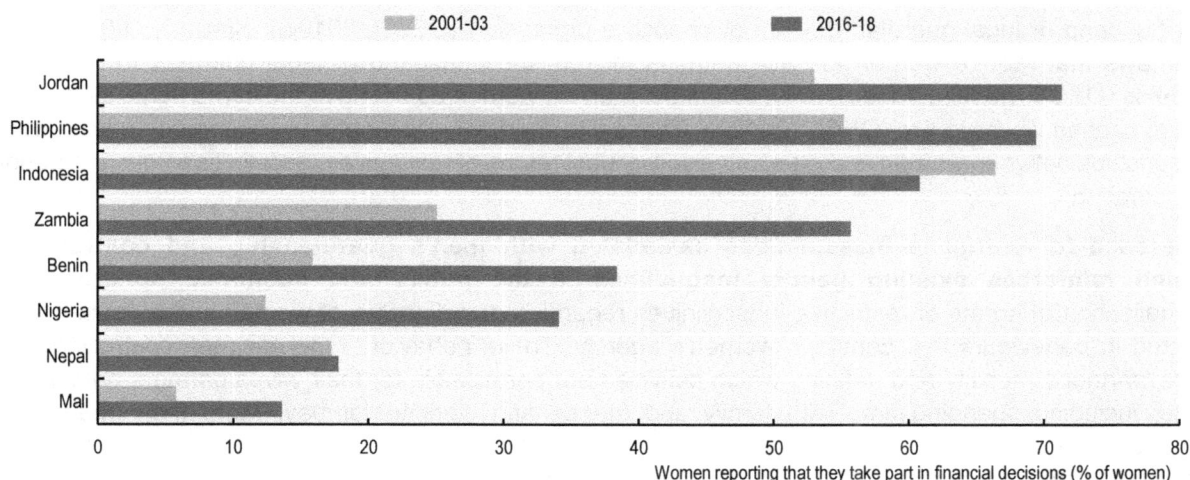

Note: Women reporting that they take part in financial decisions refers to the percentage of women who report that the main decision maker concerning large purchases is the respondent and her husband jointly. Countries are ordered by decreasing share of women that take part in financial decisions in 2016-18.
Source: (DHS, n.d.[46]), *STATcompiler*, https://www.statcompiler.com/en/.

StatLink 🔗 https://doi.org/10.1787/888934230509

4. Norms of restrictive masculinities dictate that a "real" man should protect and exercise guardianship over women in the household

Norms of restrictive masculinities promote men's role as protectors and guardians of household members, including the women in their family. Men may be expected to be guardians of female family members, which in turn underpins their power in the private sphere and echoes the belief that women need to be protected and provided for by their husband. For example, more than two-thirds of respondents in Egypt, Morocco and the Palestinian Authority believe that it is a man's duty to exercise guardianship of female relatives (El Feki, Heilman and Barker, 2017[29]). In Pakistan, guarding and controlling the women in the household – including checking their dress code and controlling their activities outside the home – are considered essential behaviours of a "real" man (Rozan, 2010[64]).

Men's guardianship role implies women's obedience. If men are expected to control women's behaviours and choices, social norms dictate that women should obey them. More than 75% of the respondents in sites across Asia and the Pacific, with the exception of the People's Republic of China (hereafter "China"), declared that a woman should obey her husband (Fulu et al., 2013[65]). Furthermore, in Egypt and Jordan, the legal framework defines wives' duty to obey their husbands in exchange for financial maintenance (OECD, 2020[66]). About 60% of respondents in Tanzania and Central Uganda declared that they believe that their community agrees with the statement: a women does not have the right to challenge her husband's opinions and decisions even if she disagrees with him (Levtov et al., 2018[41]; Vlahovicova et al., 2019[43]). Men's perceptions of their communities' beliefs are critical to understanding the way men view what is acceptable and what is expected of them by others. Indicators such as these attest to the fact that norms of masculinities are not only directed by men; rather, they are deeply intertwined with standards and social norms within a community.

This social expectation is reflected in legal frameworks. In 20 countries, married women are required by law to obey their husbands, and in 16 of these countries there are legal provisions and sanctions if women do not comply (OECD, 2019[5]). In 24 countries, the law requires women to have permission from their husband or legal guardian to work or choose a profession (OECD, 2019[5]). Similarly, 17 countries have laws that require women to have permission from their husband or legal guardian to register a business (OECD, 2019[5]). Finally, in 32 countries, married women do not have the same rights as married men to choose where to live (OECD, 2019[5]). These discriminatory laws not only reinforce unequal power relationships between women and men, but also transmit norms of restrictive masculinities from generation to generation.

Adherence to restrictive masculinities associated with men's guardianship and control over women reinforces existing gender inequalities in the public and economic spheres. The internalisation of norms of restrictive masculinities regarding guardianship of women in the household is enacted in behaviours that constrain women's agency. These behaviours include men controlling their wives'/partner's mobility and defining which activities are permissible for their wives/partners outside the home, including spending time with family and friends and working for pay. More than one-half of respondents in Azerbaijan, Tanzania and Central Uganda reported that men tell women who they can spend time with (Levtov et al., 2018[41]; UNFPA/Promundo, 2018[38]; Vlahovicova et al., 2019[43]). In Brazil, Peru and Samoa, at least 25% of female respondents reported that their husband keeps them from seeing their friends and more than 10% reported that he limits social contact with their family (WHO, 2005[67]). More than one-half of ever-married respondents in Egypt and Morocco reported that the husband controls when his wife can leave the house (El Feki, Heilman and Barker, 2017[29]). Finally, about one in five women across sites in Asia and the Pacific reported that their husband has prohibited them from working (Fulu et al., 2013[65]). These controlling behaviours are likely to reinforce existing gender inequalities in terms of access to the economic and public sphere. If men control and restrict women's mobility and activities outside the home, they may deprive women of opportunities to contribute to the family income, participate in educational programmes and/or develop social networks. For some men, restricting women's mobility may also serve as a means to maintain the traditional gender division of labour and preserve control over women's sexuality by limiting external social contact (Porter, 2011[68]).

Norms of restrictive masculinities associated with guardianship and control of women in the household can deprive women from accessing important healthcare services. Although great disparities exist across countries, data suggest that men's control over women's access to healthcare is widespread. In 8 out of 22 countries for which data are available for 2016-18, at least one in three women reported that her husband is the main decision maker regarding her healthcare (DHS, n.d.[46]). In contrast, men are more likely to have decision-making authority over their own healthcare than their female counterparts (Figure 3.5). This may have important implications for women's health. If men dominate decisions about healthcare, women may fail to have their healthcare needs met. This might be the case for several reasons. First, men may lack knowledge about the female body and hence lack the ability to make appropriate choices (Ganle and Dery, 2015[69]). Second, men might deny women access to healthcare and treatment if they oppose certain practices based on social norms; this might include examinations or treatment by male doctors and nurses. Third, men are, on average, less likely to seek preventive care and treatment (Baker et al., 2014[70]), which not only leads to insufficient uptake of healthcare services for themselves but may also lead to this being the case for their partners. Finally, if men hold decision-making authority over women's healthcare, they may choose to neglect their partners' needs if income is scarce or if they seek to spend it elsewhere. In the latter case, denial of healthcare services is inherently linked to control over financial assets (see Chapter 3, Section 3).

Figure 3.5. In most countries, women are less likely than men to have decision-making power over their access to healthcare

Percentage of women and men reporting that they are the main decision maker regarding their own healthcare

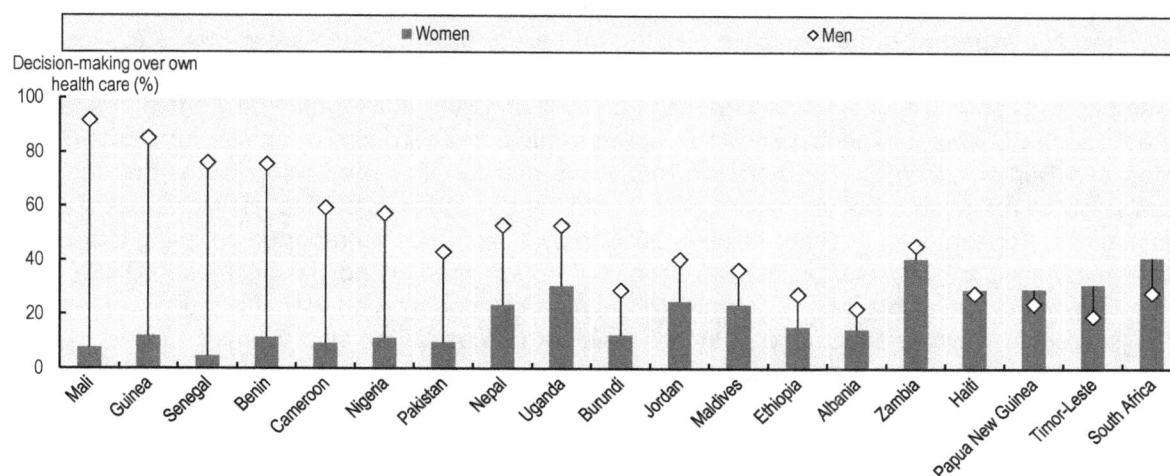

Note: Decision making over own health care refers to the percentage of respondents for whom the decision maker for their own health care is mainly the respondent. Years of data vary: Albania (2017-18), Benin (2017-18), Burundi (2016-17), Cameroon (2018), Ethiopia (2016), Guinea (2018), Haiti (2016-17), Jordan (2017-18), Maldives (2016-17), Mali (2018), Nepal (2016), Nigeria (2018), Pakistan (2017-18), Papua New Guinea (2016-18), Senegal (2018), South Africa (2016), Timor-Leste (2016), Uganda (2016), and Zambia (2018). Countries are ordered by decreasing female-to-male difference in decision making over own health care.
Source: (DHS, n.d.[46]), STATcompiler, https://www.statcompiler.com/en/.

StatLink ⫍⫎⫐ https://doi.org/10.1787/888934230528

The norm of restrictive masculinities dictating male guardianship may also drive the use of violence against women. Domestic violence may emerge as a way to reaffirm men's control over women. Large proportions of women and somewhat smaller proportions of men consider it justifiable for a husband to beat or hit his wife if she leaves the house without telling him. In ten countries for which data are available for 2016-18, more than 30% of women reported supporting this view (DHS, n.d.[46]).

Social norms that expect men to exercise authority in the home and protect female family members seem resistant to change, yet there are signs that practices are changing. In some contexts in which attitudes towards women's rights and gender equality are changing, men's authority in the private sphere and their role as the family protector is barely contested and continues to coexist with more gender-equitable attitudes and practices (Marcus, Stavropoulou and Archer-Gupta, 2018[71]; Wyrod, 2008[72]). Yet, in some countries, including Cameroon, Colombia, Haiti, Rwanda and Zambia, the proportion of ever-married women who reported that their partner insists on knowing where they are at all times decreased by at least seven percentage points between 2000 and 2018 (DHS, n.d.[46]). Moreover, the share of ever-married women reporting that their partner tries to limit their contact with their female friends also decreased in Haiti from 26% in 2007 to 19% in 2018, and in Zambia from 35% in 2000 to 25% in 2012 (DHS, n.d.[46]). Gender-equitable social norms permit both men and women to commute to distant places, develop and maintain social networks, and seek out healthcare services according to their individual needs.

5. Norms of restrictive masculinities dictate that a "real" man should dominate sexual and reproductive choices

Norms of restrictive masculinities include the expectation that "real" men have the final say in household decisions, including decisions regarding sexual activity. According to restrictive gender norms, men are expected to be proactive initiators of sexual activity, whereas women are expected to respond to their partners' needs (Dworkin et al., 2009[73]). In 2017, in the Palestinian Authority and Egypt, for example, 87% and 96% of ever-married men and 80% and 84% of ever-married women, respectively, reported that the husband expects his wife to agree to have sex with him whenever he wants (El Feki, Heilman and Barker, 2017[29]). The norms of restrictive masculinities may also lead to the denial of a woman's right to refuse to have sexual intercourse with her spouse according to her individual desire and circumstances. For example, in Timor-Leste in 2016, only 11% of women reported believing that a wife is justified in refusing to have sex with her husband if she is tired or not in the mood (DHS, n.d.[46]). Furthermore, in 2020 in China, nearly one-half (43%) of respondents reported that it is unacceptable for a woman to refuse sexual intercourse with her partner (Focus 2030 and Women Deliver, 2021[17]) (Figure 3.6). These social norms enable sexual violence, and legal frameworks can play a critical role in upholding these views; in 88 countries, the legal definition of rape does not include marital rape (OECD, 2019[5]).

Figure 3.6. In some countries, many people believe that it is unacceptable for a woman to refuse sexual intercourse with her partner

Percentage of the population finding it unacceptable for a woman to refuse sexual intercourse with her partner

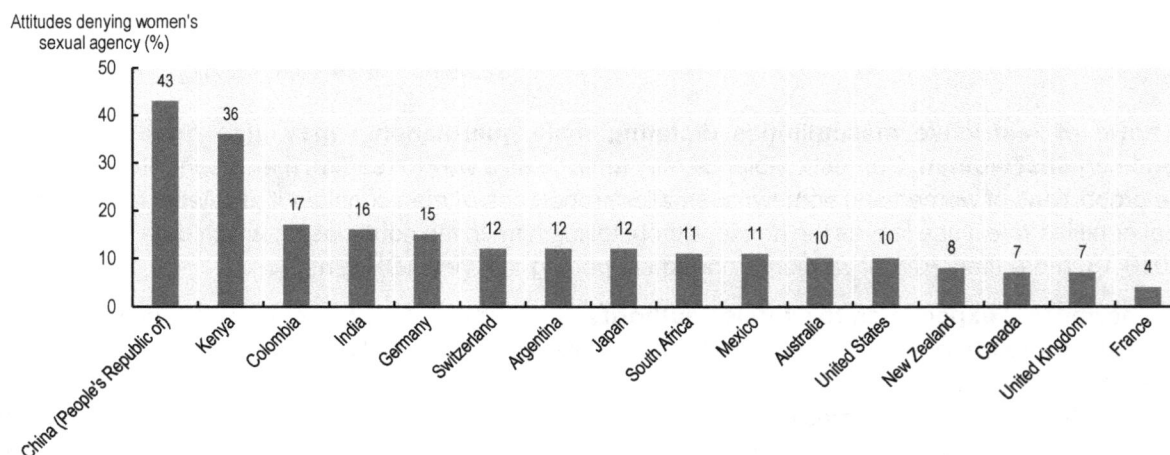

Notes: Attitudes denying women's sexual agency refers to the percentage of the population reporting that it is unacceptable for women to refuse sexual intercourse with her partner.
Source: (Focus 2030 and Women Deliver, 2021[17]), Citizens Call for a Gender-Equal World. A Roadmap for Action: Findings from a 17-Country Public Opinion Survey on Gender Equality Prepared for the Generation Equality Forum, https://womendeliver.org/wp-content/uploads/2021/02/Global_Report_English.pdf.

StatLink https://doi.org/10.1787/888934230547

Entitlement to sex with their partners may be linked to the important roles that men play in the household as breadwinners and decision makers. Men's power to decide when and how often to have sexual intercourse with their wives may be related, at least in part, to their role as financial providers. For example, in Egypt and Morocco in 2017, 33% and 36% of female respondents and 16% and 41% of male respondents, respectively, agreed that if a husband provides financially for his household, his wife is obliged to have sex with him whenever he wants (El Feki, Heilman and Barker, 2017[29]).

In addition to sexual activity, men may be expected to have the final say in reproductive decisions, including the use of contraceptives and, relatedly, choices about family size. Norms of restrictive masculinities prescribe men's control over family planning, including the use of contraception, and thus permit men to control family size, determine the timing to have children and decide whether to use condoms or not, according to their preferences (Blanc, 2001[74]; Chapagain, 2005[75]; Kabagenyi et al., 2014[76]). Controlling contraceptive use may provide a husband with a sense of power over his wife's sexuality and the ability to prevent covert extramarital affairs (Kabagenyi et al., 2014[76]; MacQuarrie et al., 2015[77]). In the Middle East and North Africa (MENA) region, for example, men enjoy greater decision-making power than women do with regard to birth control. Specifically, in Lebanon and in the Palestinian Authority in 2017, 20% and 25% of male respondents and 18% and 14% of female respondents, respectively, claimed to have sole decision-making authority over the use of contraception, while only 3% of men and women in the Palestinian Authority reported that women had the final say on contraceptive use (El Feki, Heilman and Barker, 2017[29]). In Burkina Faso in 2018, 38% of respondents reported that the husband makes decisions regarding birth spacing, while 42% reported that this decision was made jointly by the couple (OECD, 2018[11]).

When it comes to avoiding pregnancy, men are often permitted and even expected to be disengaged. While restrictive masculinities prescribe men's control over family planning, including the use of contraception, its implementation mainly rests on women's shoulders (Lohan et al., 2018[78]; MenEngage, n.d.[40]; Ruane-McAteer et al., 2020[79]). The belief that avoiding pregnancy is a woman's prerogative remains widespread and concerns the prevention of pregnancy in both stable intimate relationships and casual sexual encounters (Blanc, 2001[74]; Ekstrand et al., 2007[80]; MenEngage, n.d.[40]). In Brazil and India, for example, more than one in three men considered birth control a woman's responsibility, while as many as one-half of men in Chile and Rwanda concurred on this point (Barker et al., 2011[20]). Similarly, between 2010 and 2013, 66% of male respondents in Cambodia and 43% in urban Indonesia agreed that it is a woman's responsibility to avoid getting pregnant (Fulu et al., 2013[65]).

Norms of restrictive masculinity may perpetuate practices that undermine women's sexual agency and ability to have a safe sex life. In addition to social norms which reproduce unequal power dynamics and dictate men's control in intimate relationships, norms of restrictive masculinities promote the expectation that men should be sexually active and unambiguously heterosexual (Box 3.2) (Heilman, Barker and Harrison, 2017[3]; Greene et al., 2019[81]). Combined, these norms pose a barrier to women's reproductive autonomy and physical integrity. The combination of men's decision-making authority in intimate relationships and masculinities which encourage sexual risk-taking not only adversely affects men's sexual health, but also women's sexual experiences and ability to have a safe sex life (Greene et al., 2019[81]; Kane, Lohan and Kelly, 2018[82]).

Box 3.2. Restrictive masculinities, hypersexuality and risk-taking

Extensive sexual activity, sometimes referred to as hypersexuality is a pivotal part of restrictive masculinities. In some contexts, a "real" man is expected to frequently have heterosexual sexual intercourse and engage in multiple sexual encounters. In 2017, about 42% of male respondents in Mexico and 60% of men in the United States believed that society expects them to have multiple sexual partners, and 53% and 62%, respectively, reported that society expects them to never decline the opportunity to have sex in order to be a "real" man (Heilman, Barker and Harrison, 2017[3]). In 2011, 58% of male respondents in both India and Rwanda agreed that men are always ready to have sex and

---

that they do not talk about sex, but they just have it (Barker et al., 2011[20]). Hypersexuality is only associated with masculinity, not with femininity (Greene et al., 2019[81]).

Norms of restrictive masculinities include risk-taking and self-reliance. These norms, when enacted, can encourage men to engage in risky sexual behaviour and to refrain from preventive healthcare procedures (Blanc, 2001[74]; Ruane-McAteer et al., 2019[83]). Men who embrace restrictive masculinities have been found to be more likely to have negative attitudes towards condom use, to forego condoms during sexual intercourse, to use violence and to contract a sexually transmitted infection (Barker et al., 2010[84]; Noar and Morokoff, 2002[85]; Pulerwitz et al., 2010[86]). Those men are also reluctant to get tested for human immunodeficiency virus (HIV), pick up test results and obtain treatment (Greene et al., 2019[81]; MenEngage, n.d.[40]). Preferences for unprotected sex, combined with low take-up rates of HIV testing and treatment, reinforces high-risk sexual behaviour, undermining both men's and women's sexual health.

Norms of restrictive masculinities, combined with ideas of men's sexual entitlement, may encourage sexual violence and justify the use of physical violence. Pressure to adhere to dominant masculinities and demonstrate sexual activity undermines men's and women's sexual agency and can contribute to sexual coercion (Greene et al., 2019[81]). If men feel entitled to sex and/or seek to demonstrate their masculinity through sexual activity, they may override their partners' individual preferences, committing acts of sexual violence (Box 3.3).[5] Furthermore, societies, including both men and women, may justify cases where men resort to physical violence when their wife/partner refuses to have sex. In Guinea and Mali in 2018, for example, 48% and 63% of women, respectively, considered it justifiable for a husband to beat his wife if she refuses sexual intercourse with him (DHS, n.d.[46]). The proportion of men in these countries who hold this belief was slightly lower, standing at 25% and 23%, respectively (DHS, n.d.[46]).

Male dominance in reproductive decision making can prevent women from choosing to use contraceptives. Men's control over the use of contraception may also deny women the ability to opt for suitable contraceptive methods and increases the likelihood of covert contraceptive use (Blanc, 2001[74]). The proportions of currently married or in-union women who reported that they are not using a contraceptive method and do not intend to use one due to spousal opposition ranged from 1% in the Republic of Moldova (in 2005) to 14% in Sierra Leone (in 2008) (DHS, n.d.[46]).[6] Furthermore, in 2011, at least one in three men in Chile, India and Rwanda reported that they would be outraged if their wife asked them to use a condom (Barker et al., 2011[20]). Legal frameworks in 16 countries uphold these restrictive norms by legally requiring women pursuing the termination of a pregnancy to have the approval of the father, thus legally codifying men's final say in these decisions (OECD, 2019[5]).

Box 3.3. Sexual violence in conflict settings

Violence against women and girls represents a way to assert masculinity and demonstrate sexual virility in armed conflicts. In these settings, violence is celebrated as a heroic act and its glorification helps to encourage men to use force against vulnerable groups in order to harm their enemies and emasculate those who seek to protect them (Saferworld, 2014[87]). Sexual violence against women and girls – including rape and forced pregnancy in its most extreme forms – is used as a weapon, constituting a tactic of war (Greene, Robles and Pawlak, 2011[8]). At its core, this violence "is about gendered and patriarchal power and domination" (OECD, 2019[88]). In addition to traumatising survivors and their families, it demolishes societal structures (Reid-Cunningham, 2008[89]). Soldiers who use sexual violence may consider it a demonstration of power, strength and domination, and thus a validation of their manhood (Reid-Cunningham, 2008[89]). Furthermore, in contexts of conflict and fragility, the

---

enactment of gender-based violence – and violence more generally – is often tolerated, normalised and even celebrated (OECD, 2019[88]).

The norms of restrictive masculinities which condone male dominance in reproductive choices can have adverse consequences for women's outcomes by minimising their individual agency. Male dominance in family planning denies women equal rights to control family size and birth spacing, which has important implications for women's ability to achieve sustained livelihoods for themselves and their dependents (Nzioka, 2002[90]; Ruane-McAteer et al., 2019[83]). Social expectations about men's control in relationships and their disengagement from reproductive care pose barriers to women's ability to choose for themselves, pursue their economic ambitions and reach optimal health outcomes (Blanc, 2001[74]; Croce-Galis, Salazar and Lundgren, 2014[91]). This issue goes beyond women's control over their bodies. In light of unequal divisions of unpaid care and domestic work, women often bear the burden of childcare and are more likely to pursue ways to balance work and family life, even if this means taking low-paid, part-time and/or informal jobs (see Chapter 3, Section 1).

Gender-equitable masculinities emphasise equal partnership and respect for women's right to physical integrity. Along with these norms are practices emphasising joint decision making in partnerships, based on mutual respect and an understanding of a woman's right to make her own informed decisions regarding her own body when it comes to sexual activity, childbearing and contraceptive use. Under gender-equitable masculinities, men and boys are actively involved in sexual and reproductive choices, but in ways in which they do not dominate. In fact, these norms are already taking root. For example, in Burkina Faso in 2008, 66% of respondents reported that couples should decide jointly on the number of children to have (OECD, 2018[11]). Men who adopt gender-equitable masculinities uphold women's autonomous choices and base family planning and sexual activity on the mutual consent of informed parties. Indeed, evidence attests to the potential for change in the norms of masculinities related to sexual health and reproductive rights (Ruane-McAteer et al., 2020[79]). For example, in South Africa, the percentage of men reporting that they agreed with the statement: "A man and a woman should decide together what type of contraceptive to use" increased by more than 15 percentage points after participating in a MenCare+ programme (Olivier et al., 2016[92]).

Gender-equitable masculinities which embrace joint reproductive decision making have the potential to improve women's economic empowerment. Studies have shown that spousal communication about contraception and joint decision making play an important role in women's use of contraceptives (Ogunjuyigbe, Ojofeitimi and Liasu, 2009[93]; Yue, O'Donnell and Sparks, 2010[94]). Use of a contraceptive method is associated with higher educational attainment and labour force participation among women (Finlay and Lee, 2018[95]). Improved access to contraception can enhance women's economic outcomes through various channels: giving them the opportunity to delay their first childbearing, determine the intervals between births and limit the number of children they have according to their preferences (Finlay and Lee, 2018[95]). Changing men's openness to discussing family planning on an equal footing with their wives/partners may thus improve women's empowerment opportunities.

References

Ahmed, F. (2008), "Microcredit, men, and masculinity", *NWSA Journal*, Vol. 20/2, pp. 122-155, https://muse.jhu.edu/article/246760/summary. [57]

Akilova, M. and Y. Marti (2014), "What is the Effect of Women's Financial Empowerment on Intimate Partner Violence in Jordan?", *Global Social Welfare*, Vol. 1, pp. 65–74, https://doi.org/10.1007/s40609-014-0005-x. [63]

Amin, M., A. Islam and A. Sakhonchik (2016), "Does Paternity Leave Matter for Female Employment in Developing Economies? Evidence from Firm", *World Bank Policy Research Working Paper*, Vol. 7588, https://ssrn.com/abstract=2740841. [25]

Anderson, D. and D. Saunders (2003), "Leaving an Abusive Partner: An Empirical Review of Predictors, the Process of Leaving, and Psychological Well-Being", *Trauma, Violence, & Abuse*, Vol. 4/2, https://journals.sagepub.com/doi/pdf/10.1177/1524838002250769. [62]

Baker, P. et al. (2014), "The men's health gap: men must be included in the global health equity agenda", *WHO Bulletin* 92, https://www.who.int/bulletin/volumes/92/8/13-132795/en/. [70]

Bannon, I. and M. Correia (2006), *The Other Half of Gender*, The World Bank, Washington, D.C., http://openknowledge.worldbank.org/handle/10986/7029. [49]

Barker, G. (2007), *The role of men and boys in achieving gender equality*, https://www.un.org/womenwatch/daw/public/w2000/W2000%20Men%20and%20Boys%20E%20web.pdf. [34]

Barker, G. et al. (2011), *Evolving Men: Initial Results from the International Men and Gender Equality Survey (IMAGES)*, https://www.icrw.org/wp-content/uploads/2016/10/Evolving-Men-Initial-Results-from-the-International-Men-and-Gender-Equality-Survey-IMAGES-1.pdf. [20]

Barker, G. et al. (2010), "Questioning gender norms with men to improve health outcomes: Evidence of impact", *Global Public Health*, https://xyonline.net/sites/xyonline.net/files/Barker%2C%20Questioning%20gender%20norms%20with%20men%202010.pdf. [84]

Bittman, M. et al. (2003), "When Does Gender Trump Money? Bargaining and Time in Household Work", *American Journal of Sociology*, Vol. 109/1, pp. 186-214, https://www.jstor.org/stable/10.1086/378341?seq=1. [9]

Blanc, A. (2001), "The Effect of Power in Sexual Relationships on Sexual and Reproductive Health: An Examination of the Evidence", *Studies in Family Planning*, Vol. 32/3, pp. 189-213, https://onlinelibrary.wiley.com/doi/pdf/10.1111/j.1728-4465.2001.00189.x. [74]

Browning, M. and P. Chiappori (1998), "Efficient Intra-Household Allocations: A General Characterization and Empirical Tests", *Econometrica*, Vol. 66/6, pp. 1241–1278, http://www.jstor.org/stable/2999616. [15]

Cederström, C. (2019), *State of Nordic Fathers*, Promundo, Nordic Council of Ministers, MÄN, Copenhagen, https://promundoglobal.org/state-of-nordic-fathers-report-identifies-possible-avenues-to-increase-fathers-share-of-childcare-and-leave/?_ga=2.256281667.996431202.1605524549-11648403.1592395010. [39]

Chapagain, M. (2005), "Masculine interest behind high prevalence of female contraceptive methods in rural Nepal", *Australian Journal of Rural Health*, Vol. 13/1, pp. 35-42, http://10.1111/j.1440-1854.2004.00643.x. [75]

Croce-Galis, M., E. Salazar and R. Lundgren (2014), *Male engagement in family planning: Reducing unmet need for family planning by addressing gender norms*, IRH, https://irh.org/wp-content/uploads/2014/10/Male_Engagement_in_FP_Brief_10.10.14.pdf. [91]

Dahl, G., K. Løken and M. Mogstad (2014), "Peer Effects in Program Participation", *American Economic Review*, Vol. 104/7, pp. 2049-2074, http://dx.doi.org/10.1257/aer.104.7.2049. [21]

DHS (n.d.), *STATcompiler*, https://www.statcompiler.com/en/. [46]

Dolan, C. (2003), *Collapsing Masculinities and Weak States—A Case Study of Northern Uganda*, Zed Books, London, https://www.researchgate.net/publication/284885804_Collapsing_masculinities_and_weak_states_A_case_study_of_Northern_Uganda. [48]

Doyle, K. et al. (2018), "Gender-transformative Bandebereho couples' intervention to promote male engagement in reproductive and maternal health and violence prevention in Rwanda: Findings from a randomized controlled trial", *PLoS ONE*, Vol. 13/4, https://doi.org/10.1371/journal.pone.0192756. [35]

Dworkin, S. et al. (2009), "Gendered empowerment and HIV prevention: Policy and programmatic pathways to success in the MENA region", *Journal of Acquired Immune Deficiency Syndromes*, Vol. 51/SUPPL. 3, p. S111, https://www.ncbi.nlm.nih.gov/pmc/articles/PMC3329725/. [73]

Ekstrand, M. et al. (2007), "Preventing pregnancy: A girls' issue. Seventeen-year-old Swedish boys' perceptions on abortion, reproduction and use of contraception", *European Journal of Contraception and Reproductive Health Care*, Vol. 12/2, pp. 111-118, https://www.tandfonline.com/doi/abs/10.1080/13625180701201145?journalCode=iejc20. [80]

El Feki, S., B. Heilman and G. Barker (2017), *Understanding Masculinities: Results from the International Men and Gender Equality Survey (IMAGES) - Middle East and North Africa*, UN Women, Cairo and Promundo-US, Washington, D.C., https://www.unwomen.org/en/digital-library/publications/2017/5/understanding-masculinities-results-from-the-images-in-the-middle-east-and-north-africa. [29]

Elliott, K. (2015), "Caring Masculinities: Theorizing an Emerging Concept", *Men and Masculinities*, doi: 10.1177/1097184X15576203, pp. 240-259, https://doi.org/10.1177%2F1097184X15576203. [7]

Eurobarometer (2017), *Special Eurobarometer 465: Gender Equality 2017*, http://data.europa.eu/euodp/en/data/dataset/S2154_87_4_465_ENG. [18]

Ferrant, G., L. Pesando and K. Nowacka (2014), *Unpaid Care Work: The missing link in the anaylsis of gender gaps in labour outcomes*, OECD Development Centre, Paris, https://www.oecd.org/dev/development-gender/Unpaid_care_work.pdf. [32]

Ferrant, G. and A. Thim (2016), "Measuring Women's Economic Empowerment: Time Use Data and Gender Inequality", *OECD Development Policy Papers* 16, p. 23, https://www.oecd.org/dev/development-gender/MEASURING-WOMENS-ECONOMIC-EMPOWERMENT-Gender-Policy-Paper-No-16.pdf. [31]

Finlay, J. and M. Lee (2018), "Identifying Causal Effects of Reproductive Health Improvements on Women's Economic Empowerment Through the Population Poverty Research Initiative", *The Milbank Quarterly*, Vol. 96/2, pp. 300-322, https://www.ncbi.nlm.nih.gov/pmc/articles/PMC5987803/. [95]

Focus 2030 and Women Deliver (2021), *Citizens Call for a Gender-Equal World. A Roadmap for Action: Findings from a 17-Country Public Opinion Survey on Gender Equality Prepared for the Generation Equality Forum*, https://womendeliver.org/wp-content/uploads/2021/02/Global_Report_English.pdf. [17]

Fulu, E. et al. (2013), *Why do some men use violence against women and how can we prevent it? Quantitative findings from the United Nations multi-country study on men and violence in Asia and the Pacific*, UNDP, UNFPA, UN Women and UNV, Bangkok, https://docs.google.com/viewer?embedded=true&url=http%3A%2F%2Fwww.partners4prevention.org%2Fsites%2Fdefault%2Ffiles%2Fresources%2Fp4p-report.pdf. [65]

Ganle, J. and I. Dery (2015), "'What men don't know can hurt women's health': a qualitative study of the barriers to and opportunities for men's involvement in maternal healthcare in Ghana", *Reproductive Health*, Vol. 12/1, p. 93, https://reproductive-health-journal.biomedcentral.com/articles/10.1186/s12978-015-0083-y. [69]

Greene, M. et al. (2019), *Getting to Equal Men, Gender Equality, and Sexual and Reproductive Health and Rights*, Promundo-US, Washington, D.C., https://promundoglobal.org/resources/getting-to-equal-men-gender-equality-and-sexual-and-reproductive-health-and-rights/#:~:text=Through%20a%20review%20and%20analysis,crucial%20to%20achieving%20SRHR%20for. [81]

Greene, M., O. Robles and P. Pawlak (2011), *Masculinities, Social Change, and Development*, The World Bank, Washington, D.C., https://www.alignplatform.org/resources/masculinities-social-change-and-development. [8]

Greenstein, T. (2000), *Economic dependence, gender, and the division of labor in the home: A replication and extension*, National Council on Family Relations, https://onlinelibrary.wiley.com/doi/full/10.1111/j.1741-3737.2000.00322.x. [28]

Hanlon, N. (2012), *Masculinities, Care and Equality: Identity and Nurture in Men's Lives*, Palgrave Macmillan, New York. [16]

Hegewisch, A. and J. Gornick (2011), "The impact of work-family policies on women's employment: a review of research from OECD countries", *Community, Work & Family*, Vol. 14/2, pp. 119-138, http://dx.doi.org/10.1080/13668803.2011.571395. [33]

Heilman, B., G. Barker and A. Harrison (2017), *The Man Box: A Study on Being a Young Man in the US, UK, and Mexico*, Promundo-US, Washington, D.C. and Unilever, London, https://promundoglobal.org/resources/man-box-study-young-man-us-uk-mexico/. [3]

Hung, A., J. Yoong and E. Brown (2012), "Empowering Women Through Financial Awareness and Education", *OECD Working Papers on Finance, Insurance and Private Pensions*, Vol. 14, https://www.oecd-ilibrary.org/docserver/5k9d5v6kh56g-en.pdf?expires=1608121562&id=id&accname=ocid84004878&checksum=88EF4197B87A059D3D6041935DD897D3. [53]

Hunter, S., D. Riggs and M. Augoustinos (2017), "Hegemonic masculinity versus a caring masculinity: Implications for understanding primary caregiving fathers", *Social and Personality Psychology Compass*, Vol. 11/3, p. e12307, https://onlinelibrary.wiley.com/doi/pdf/10.1111/spc3.12307. [47]

Ipsos (2019), *International Women's Day 2019: Global Attitudes towards Gender Equality*, https://www.ipsos.com/sites/default/files/ct/news/documents/2019-03/international-womens-day-2019-global-attitudes-towards-gender-equality.pdf. [22]

Johansson, T. (2011), "Fatherhood in Transition: Paternity Leave and Changing Masculinities", *Journal of Family Communication*, Vol. 11/3, pp. 165-180, https://doi.org/10.1080/15267431.2011.561137. [37]

Johnson, N. et al. (2016), "Gender, Assets, and Agricultural Development: Lessons from Eight Projects", *World Development*, Vol. 83, pp. 295-311, http://dx.doi.org/10.1016/j.worlddev.2016.01.009. [54]

Kabagenyi, A. et al. (2014), "Barriers to male involvement in contraceptive uptake and reproductive health services: A qualitative study of men and women's perceptions in two rural districts in Uganda", *Reproductive Health*, Vol. 11/1, pp. 1-9, https://link.springer.com/article/10.1186/1742-4755-11-21. [76]

Kane, J., M. Lohan and C. Kelly (2018), "Adolescent men's attitudes and decision making in relation to pregnancy and pregnancy outcomes: An integrative review of the literature from 2010 to 2017", *Journal of Adolescence*, Vol. 72, pp. 23-31, https://doi.org/10.1016/j.adolescence.2018.12.008. [82]

Kim, J. et al. (2009), "Assessing the incremental effects of combining economic and health interventions: The IMAGE study in South Africa", *Bulletin of the World Health Organization*, Vol. 87/11, pp. 824-832, https://www.who.int/bulletin/volumes/87/11/08-056580/en/. [60]

Kimmel, M., J. Hearn and R. Connell (2005), *Handbook of Studies on Men and Masculinities*, SAGE Publications, Thousand Oaks. [36]

Latshaw, B. and S. Hale (2016), "'The domestic handoff': stay-at-home fathers' time-use in female breadwinner families", *Journal of Family Studies*, Vol. 22/2, pp. 97-120, https://www.tandfonline.com/doi/full/10.1080/13229400.2015.1034157. [12]

Levtov, R. et al. (2018), *Momentum Toward Equality: Results from the International Men and Gender Equality Survey (IMAGES) in Tanzania*, Promundo-US, Uzazi na Malezi Bora Tanzania, and Tanzania Commission for AIDS, https://promundoglobal.org/wp-content/uploads/2018/10/Momentum-Toward-Equality-IMAGES-Tanzania-Report-EN-POSTPRINT-2.25.19.pdf. [41]

Lohan, M. et al. (2018), "Can teenage men be targeted to prevent teenage pregnancy? A feasibility cluster randomised controlled intervention trial in schools", *Prevention Science*, pp. 1-12, https://doi.org/10.1007/s11121-018-0928-z. [78]

Lund, R., S. Meriläinen and J. Tienari (2019), "New masculinities in universities? Discourses, ambivalence and potential change", *Gender, Work & Organization*, Vol. 26/10, pp. 1376-1397, http://dx.doi.org/10.1111/gwao.12383. [23]

MacQuarrie, K. et al. (2015), *Contraception: Trends in Attitudes and Use.*, ICF International, Rockville. [77]

Manley, J. and V. Slavchevska (2016), "Are Cash Transfers the Answer for Children in Sub-Saharan Africa? A Literature Review", *12*, No. 2016, Towson University Department of Economics, http://webapps.towson.edu/cbe/economics/workingpapers/2016-12.pdf. [59]

Marcus, R., M. Stavropoulou and N. Archer-Gupta (2018), *Programming with adolescent boys to promote gender-equitable masculinities*, Gender and Adolescence: Global Evidence (GAGE), https://www.gage.odi.org/wp-content/uploads/2018/12/GAGE-Masculinities-Policy-Brief-WEB.pdf. [71]

MenEngage (n.d.), *Men, Masculinities, and Changing Power: A Discussion Paper on Engaging Men in Gender Equality From Beijing 1995 to 2015*, http://www.unfpa.org/sites/default/files/resource-pdf/Men-Masculinities-and-Changing-Power-MenEngage-2014.pdf. [40]

Nikiforidis, L. et al. (2017), "Do Mothers Spend More on Daughters While Fathers Spend More on Sons?", *Journal of Consumer Psychology*, Vol. 28/1, pp. 149-156, http://dx.doi.org/10.1002/jcpy.1004. [56]

Njuki, J. and P. Sanginga (2013), *Women, livestock ownership and markets: Bridging the gender gap in eastern and southern Africa*, Routledge, London, https://cgspace.cgiar.org/handle/10568/34088. [51]

Noar, S. and P. Morokoff (2002), "The Relationship Between Masculinity Ideology, Condom Attitudes, and Condom Use Stage of Change: A Structural Equation Modeling Approach", *International Journal of Men's Health*, Vol. 1/1, pp. 43-58, https://d1wqtxts1xzle7.cloudfront.net/44664511/The_relationship_between_masculinity_ide20160412-12968-14zkdtx.pdf?1460480222=&response-content-disposition=inline%3B+filename%3DThe_Relationship_Between_Masculinity_Ide.pdf&Expires=1597687337&Signature=Frjxm. [85]

Nzioka, C. (2002), *Programming for Male Involvement in Reproductive Health. Report of the Meeting of WHO Regional Advisors in Reproductive Health.*, WHO Press, https://www.who.int/reproductivehealth/publications/general/WHO_RHR_02_3/en/. [90]

OECD (2020), "COVID-19 crisis in the MENA region: impact on gender equality and policy responses", *OECD Policy Responses to Coronavirus (COVID-19(*, https://www.oecd.org/coronavirus/policy-responses/covid-19-crisis-in-the-mena-region-impact-on-gender-equality-and-policy-responses-ee4cd4f4/#section-d1e240. [66]

OECD (2020), *OECD Family Database*, OECD, http://www.oecd.org/social/family/database.htm. [19]

OECD (2020), *Over the Rainbow? The Road to LGBTI Inclusion*, OECD Publishing, Paris, https://dx.doi.org/10.1787/8d2fd1a8-en. [4]

OECD (2019), "Engaging with men and masculinities in fragile and conflict-affected states", *OECD Development Policy Papers*, No. 17, OECD Publishing, Paris, https://dx.doi.org/10.1787/36e1bb11-en. [88]

OECD (2019), *Gender, Institutions and Development Database (GID-DB)*, OECD, https://oe.cd/ds/GIDDB2019 (accessed on 18 May 2020). [27]

OECD (2019), *Part-time and Partly Equal: Gender and Work in the Netherlands*, OECD Publishing, Paris, https://dx.doi.org/10.1787/204235cf-en. [26]

OECD (2019), *SIGI 2019 Global Report: Transforming Challenges into Opportunities*, Social Institutions and Gender Index, OECD Publishing, Paris, https://dx.doi.org/10.1787/bc56d212-en. [5]

OECD (2019), *Society at a Glance 2019: OECD Social Indicators*, OECD Publishing, Paris, https://dx.doi.org/10.1787/soc_glance-2019-en. [2]

OECD (2018), *Burkin Faso Etude Pays SIGI*, OECD Development Centre, http://www.oecd.org/development/development-gender/ETUDE-PAYS-SIGI-BURKINA-FASO.pdf. [11]

OECD (2016), *Background brief on fathers' leave and its use*, OECD Publishing, https://www.oecd.org/els/family/Backgrounder-fathers-use-of-leave.pdf. [24]

OECD (2015), *Uganda SIGI Country Report*, OECD Development Centre, http://www.oecd.org/dev/development-gender/The%20Uganda%20SIGI%20Country%20Study.pdf. [50]

Ogunjuyigbe, P., E. Ojofeitimi and A. Liasu (2009), "Spousal communication, changes in partner attitude, and contraceptive use among the Yorubas of Southwest Nigeria", *Indian Journal of Community Medicine*, Vol. 34/2, pp. 112-116, https://europepmc.org/article/med/19966956. [93]

Olivier, D. et al. (2016), *MenCare+ South Africa Outcome Measurement Report*, https://men-care.org/wp-content/uploads/sites/3/2016/07/MCSA-Outcome-Measurement-Report.pdf. [92]

Porter, G. (2011), "'I think a woman who travels a lot is befriending other men and that's why she travels': mobility constraints and their implications for rural women and girls in sub-Saharan Africa", *Gender, Place and Culture*, Vol. 18/1, https://www.tandfonline.com/doi/full/10.1080/0966369X.2011.535304. [68]

Postmus, J. et al. (2020), "Economic Abuse as an Invisible Form of Domestic Violence: A Multicountry Review", *Trauma, Violence, & Abuse*, Vol. 21/2, https://doi.org/10.1177%2F1524838018764160. [61]

Pulerwitz, J. et al. (2010), "Addressing Gender Dynamics and Engaging Men in HIV Programs: Lessons Learned from Horizons Research", *Public Health Reports*, Vol. 125/2, https://journals.sagepub.com/doi/10.1177/003335491012500219. [86]

Quisumbing, A. and J. Maluccio (2000), "Intrahousehold allocation and gender relations: new empirical evidence from four developing countries", *FCND Discussion Paper*, pp. 1-80, https://www.ifpri.org/publication/intrahousehold-allocation-and-gender-relations. [55]

Reid-Cunningham, A. (2008), "Rape as a Weapon of Genocide", *Genocide Studies and Prevention: An International Journal*, Vol. 3/3, https://scholarcommons.usf.edu/gsp/vol3/iss3/4. [89]

Rozan (2010), *Understanding Masculinities: A Formative Research on Masculinities and Gender based Violence in a peri-urban area in Rawalpindi, Pakistan*, Rozan, Partners for Prevention, ICRW, http://menengage.org/wp-content/uploads/2014/06/Understanding_Masculinities.pdf. [64]

Ruane-McAteer, E. et al. (2019), "Interventions addressing men, masculinities and gender equality in sexual and reproductive health and rights: an evidence and gap map and systematic review of reviews", *BMJ Global Health*, Vol. 4/5, http://dx.doi.org/10.1136/bmjgh-2019-001634. [83]

Ruane-McAteer, E. et al. (2020), "Gender-transformative programming with men and boys to improve sexual and reproductive health and rights: a systematic review of intervention studies", *BMJ Global Health*, Vol. 5, https://gh.bmj.com/content/5/10/e002997. [79]

Saferworld (2014), *Masculinities, conflict and peacebuilding: Perspectives on men through a gender lens*, https://www.saferworld.org.uk/downloads/pubdocs/masculinities-conflict-and-peacebuilding.pdf. [87]

Sanders, C. (2015), "Economic Abuse in the Lives of Women Abused by an Intimate Partner: A Qualitative Study", *Violence Against Women*, Vol. 21/1, pp. 3-29, https://journals.sagepub.com/doi/full/10.1177/1077801214564167. [58]

Segal, L. (1993), "Changing Men: Masculinitities in Context", *Theory and Society*, Vol. 22/5, pp. 625-641, http://www.jstor.org/stable/657987. [6]

Sevilla-Sanz, A., J. Gimenez-Nadal and C. Fernández (2010), "Gender Roles and the Division of Unpaid Work in Spanish Households", *Feminist Economics*, Vol. 16/4, pp. 137-184, https://www.tandfonline.com/doi/full/10.1080/13545701.2010.531197. [13]

Spindler, E. et al. (2019), *Child marriage, fertility, and family planning in Niger: Results from a study inspired by the International Men and Gender Equality Survey (IMAGES)*, Promundo-US, Washington DC, https://promundoglobal.org/wp-content/uploads/2019/02/IMAGES-NIGER-Full-Report-Web-006.pdf. [42]

Thébaud, S. (2010), "Masculinity, Bargaining, and Breadwinning: Understanding Men's Housework in the Cultural Context of Paid Work", *Gender & Society*, Vol. 24/3, pp. 330-354, http://dx.doi.org/10.1177/0891243210369105. [10]

UBS (2019), *Own your worth*, UBS, Zurich, http://www.ubs.com/global/en/wealth-management/our-approach/investor-watch/2019/own-your-worth.html?campID=CAAS-ActivityStream. [52]

Uchendu, E. (2009), *Masculinities in Contemporary Africa*, African Books Collective, Oxford, https://muse.jhu.edu/book/16940. [14]

UNFPA Ukraine (2018), *Masculinity today: Men's attitudes towards gender stereotypes and violence against women*, UNFPA, Kyiv, https://promundoglobal.org/wp-content/uploads/2018/06/Masculinity-Today-Mens_Report.pdf. [44]

UNFPA/Promundo (2018), *Engaging Men in Unpaid Care Work: An advocacy brief for Eastern Europe*, UNFPA, Istanbul and Promundo, Washington, D.C., https://eeca.unfpa.org/en/publications/engaging-men-unpaid-care-work. [38]

UNFPA/SCFWCA (2018), *Gender equality and gender relations in Azerbaijan: current trends and opportunities. Findings from the Men and Gender Equality Survey (IMAGES)*, UNFPA Azerbaijan, Baku, https://promundoglobal.org/wp-content/uploads/2018/12/IMAGES-Azerbaijan-report.pdf. [45]

Valfort, M. (2017), "LGBTI in OECD Countries: A Review", *OECD Social, Employment and Migration Working Papers*, No. 198, OECD Publishing, Paris, https://dx.doi.org/10.1787/d5d49711-en. [1]

van der Gaag, N. et al. (2019), *State of the World's Fathers: Unlocking the Power of Men's Care*, Promundo-US, Washington, DC, https://men-care.org/wp-content/uploads/sites/3/2019/06/SOWF-2019_006_WEB.pdf. [30]

Vlahovicova, K. et al. (2019), *Evolving Perspectives: Results from the International Men and Gender Equality Survey (IMAGES) in Central Uganda*, Promundo-US and International Center for Research on Women, Washington DC, https://promundoglobal.org/wp-content/uploads/2019/05/BLS18278_PRO_IMAGES_REPORT_UGANDA_WEB_FINAL-updated2.pdf. [43]

WHO (2005), *WHO multi-country study on women's health and domestic violence against women*, WHO, Geneva, https://www.who.int/reproductivehealth/publications/violence/24159358X/en/. [67]

Wyrod, R. (2008), "Between Women's Rights and Men's Authority", *Gender & Society*, Vol. 22/6, http://dx.doi.org/10.1177/0891243208325888. [72]

Yue, K., C. O'Donnell and P. Sparks (2010), "The effect of spousal communication on contraceptive use in Central Terai, Nepal", *Patient Education and Counseling*, Vol. 81/3, pp. 402-408, https://pubmed.ncbi.nlm.nih.gov/20719462/. [94]

Notes

[1] For a list of countries/territories included in all surveys referenced in this publication please see the Annex.

[2] Belgium, Luxembourg and Spain.

[3] Data for this indicator were collected over the course of multiple years between 2009 and 2019.

[4] The size of the sample in each of these countries is unknown, and thus should not be taken to be representative. For more information on the methodology used for this research, see: https://www.ubs.com/global/en/media/display-page-ndp/en-20190306-financial-security.html.

[5] In conflict settings, restrictive norms that link masculinity to sexual virility, and glorify violence, serve to encourage sexual assault and rape as a weapon of war (Box 3.3).

[6] Data are available for 45 countries between 2005 and 2010.

4 Measuring progress towards gender-equitable masculinities

This chapter highlights the need for more data on masculinities to inform policy making. In order to facilitate the creation of an evidence base on the status of masculine norms, it proposes a list of indicators to measure each of the ten norms of restrictive masculinities presented in Chapter 2 and Chapter 3. Each list includes both currently available and ideal indicators that assess masculine norms based on laws, attitudes and social practices. The aim of this chapter is to guide future data collection efforts that can create a comparable and robust evidence base to support programmes and policies to promote gender-equitable masculine norms.

In order to address restrictive masculinities, policy makers need the right data

Monitoring social change towards more gender-equitable masculinities requires the right indicators to pinpoint challenges and track progress. Data and evidence have been an important part of the gender equality agenda. With the right data, policy makers and other stakeholders can identify the main challenges, design effective policies and programmes, and understand the relationships between legal frameworks, social norms and women's outcomes. In doing so, data allow them to monitor the impact of policies, legal reforms and programmes, and the same can be true when it comes to shifting masculinities, provided that the right data are available.

The right data for monitoring progress towards gender-equitable masculinities should allow insights into the attitudes, practices and legal frameworks that signal declining acceptance of restrictive masculinities. Attitudinal data should measure a decrease in the percentage of the population – including both women and men – that supports gender-inequitable statements and behaviours. Moreover, as individual men must navigate these norms and, in doing so, have opportunities to choose whether to adopt or reject these norms, it is important to understand how they see the risks of not conforming to these dominant ideals. In order to measure these views, there is a need for indicators that assess men's perceptions of their communities' beliefs. However, these attitudinal variables may not be enough to understand how widespread norms of restrictive masculinities are. As such, these data should be accompanied by indicators of the prevalence of harmful practices – such as violence against women – and outcomes data indicating gender imbalances, such as the percentage of women in parliaments. Finally, indicators assessing legal frameworks add another layer of insight. Laws can not only reflect the social norms governing a society, but they can also create constraints and opportunities when it comes to the behaviours of men and women that may uphold restrictive masculinities. For instance, legal frameworks that do not permit women to be heads of household send a clear message that men are, by default, the decision makers in households.

Using a combination of available data and proposals for new indicators, this chapter proposes a list of indicators to guide efforts to measure progress towards changing masculinities. Specifically, this chapter suggests a list of indicators that policy makers can currently use to track progress in transforming masculinities across the ten defining norms described in Chapters 2 and 3, presented in Table 4.1. Each table contains indicators to measure laws, attitudes associated with restrictive masculinities, and the consequences of these norms for women and girls (Table 4.2 to Table 4.11). Each table includes "ideal" indicators identified to best measure progress; however, as there are very few available ideal indicators, and those which are available are limited by low country coverage, tracking progress towards gender-equitable masculinities at present remains limited. As such, each table also includes a list of currently available indicators. In doing so, the tables provide a way forward for future data collection efforts to identify and measure the status of masculinities and their impact on women's empowerment across countries at the global level.

These lists of indicators reveal and respond to critical data gaps and important asymmetries between developing and developed countries. First, there are more data available on gender norms in the private sphere in developing countries, whereas in developed countries most of the available data on gender norms and norms of restrictive masculinities focus on the economic and public sphere. Second, there are more data available on gender-equitable masculinities in developed countries. This risks giving the impression that gender-equitable masculinities originate or exist only in developed countries. Both of these trends in the data point to the pressing need for a universal measurement that, on the one hand, recognises both the public and private spheres as sites of norms of masculinities, and on the other hand, allows for the measurement of progress towards gender-equitable masculinities in a comparable manner across developed and developing countries.

Table 4.1. The ten defining norms of restrictive masculinities

Economic and political spheres	Private sphere
Norms of restrictive masculinities say a "real" man should:	
Be the breadwinner	Not to unpaid care and domestic work
Be financially dominant	Have the final say in household decisions
Work in "manly" jobs	Control household assets
Be the "ideal worker"	Protect and exercise guardianship
Be a "manly" leader	Dominate sexual and reproductive choices

Note: This is not an exhaustive list of all norms of restrictive masculinities. The objective in the creation of this list was to account for those norms which have the most significant, and direct impact on the empowerment of women and girls.

The data presented below permit important analysis of the mechanisms of norms of masculinities. For example, a correlation analysis of available indicators reveals that restrictive masculinities are self-reinforcing, whereas this is not the case for gender-equitable masculinities. In this analysis, two types of indicators were used: i) indicators measuring the percentage of the population agreeing with norms of restrictive masculinities, and ii) indicators measuring the percentage of the population supporting gender-equitable masculinities. Indeed, the correlation among the first set of indicators is higher and much more significant than among the second. This means that where some norms of restrictive masculinities are widely accepted, other norms of restrictive masculinities are as well. For example, where the norm that men are breadwinners is widespread, the other norms listed in this report are likely also widespread. Conversely, when a norm of gender-equitable masculinities is widely supported by the population, others are not necessarily also widely accepted. Findings such as these rely on the availability of quality data and provide interesting results to be considered in policy making and programming.

Table 4.2. Be the breadwinner

Indicators tracking progress towards gender-equitable masculine norms

	Indicators	Country coverage	Year	Data source
Ideal indicators				
Legal framework	Number of countries with legal frameworks mandating non-discrimination on the basis of sex in employment	180	2009-19	SIGI
Attitudes	Percentage of the population agreeing with the following statement: Men should really be the ones to bring money home to provide for their families, not women	-	-	-
	Percentage of the population agreeing with the following statement: A man who stays at home to look after his children is less of a man	27	2019	Ipsos
	Percentage of the population agreeing with the following statement: In my community, it is important that men are the ones who make money to provide for their families, not women	-	-	-
Consequences for women's empowerment	Female labour force participation and employment rates	141	2010-20	ILO
	Prevalence of female informal employment	38	2010-19	ILO
	Percentage of low-paid workers, among all low-paid workers, who are female	54	2010-19	ILO
Available indicators				
Legal framework	-	-	-	-
Attitudes	Percentage of the population agreeing with the following statement: When jobs are scarce, men should have more right to a job than women	49	1990/94-2017/20	WVS
	Percentage of the population agreeing with the following statement: The most important role of a man is to earn money	28	2017	Eurobarometer
	Percentage of the population agreeing with the following statement: Responsibility for providing financial support to the family rests with the husband [*]	12	2015	IMAGES (Promundo)
	Percentage of the population agreeing with the following statement: It is a man's job to earn money and a woman's job to take care of the home and family	2	2017/20	WVS (gender module)
	Percentage of the population agreeing with the following statement: Men should support their family financially in order to be good husbands/partners	1	2017	Pew Research Center
Consequences for women's empowerment	-	-	-	-

Note: Data on this indicator marked with [*] have been collected in 12 countries using slightly different wording. Information on IMAGES data will be completed after Promundo's IMAGES Optimisation process.

Table 4.3. Be financially dominant

Indicators tracking progress towards gender-equitable masculine norms

	Indicators	Country coverage	Year	Data source
Ideal indicators				
Legal framework	Number of countries with a legal framework mandating equal remuneration for work of equal value	190	1971-2020	WBL
Attitudes	Percentage of the population agreeing with the following statement: If a women earns more money than her husband, it's almost certain to cause problems	49	1995/98-2017/20	WVS
	Percentage of the population considering it acceptable that in some circumstances, a woman is paid less than a male colleague for the same job	-	-	-
	Percentage of the population agreeing with the following statement: Men should earn more than their spouse	-	-	-
	Percentage of the population agreeing with the following statement: In my community, a man who earns less than his wife will be judged	-	-	-
	Percentage of the population agreeing with the following statement: Men should earn more than their female colleagues	-	-	-
Consequences for women's empowerment	Gender wage gap by occupation	39	2010-20	ILO
	Representation of women in managerial positions	161	2010-19	ILO
	Representation of women in senior and middle management positions	108	2010-19	ILO
	Representation of women on company boards	57	2016-20	MSCI
	Percentage of women reporting that they take part in the decision-making process at home	-	-	-
Available indicators				
Legal framework	-	-	-	-
Attitudes	Percentage considering it acceptable that in some circumstances, a woman is paid less than a male colleague for the same job	28	2017	Eurobarometer
	Percentage of the population finding it acceptable that women earn less than men for the same work	17	2021	Focus 2030 and Women Deliver
	Percentage of the population agreeing with the following statement: When jobs are scarce, men should have more right to a job than women	49	1990/94-2017/20	WVS
Consequences for women's empowerment	Percentage of women for whom the decision-maker regarding major household purchases is mainly the husband	70	1999-2018	DHS

Table 4.4. Work in "manly" jobs

Indicators tracking progress towards gender-equitable masculine norms

	Indicators	Country coverage	Year	Data source
Ideal indicators				
Legal framework	Number of countries where the legal framework does not allow women to work in jobs deemed dangerous in the same way as men	190	1971-2020	WBL
	Number of countries where the legal framework does not allow women to work in the same industries as men	190	1971-2020	WBL
Attitudes	Percentage of the population agreeing with the following statement: A man who works in "feminine jobs", such as a nurse, nanny, teacher, etc., is less of a man	-	-	-
	Percentage of the population agreeing with the following statement: In my community, if men work in "feminine jobs", such as a nurse, nanny, teacher, etc., they are/would be judged	-	-	-
	Percentage of the population associating some jobs as feminine or masculine, not as gender neutral	2	2020	SIGI country studies
Consequences for women's empowerment	Representation of women as heads of states (presidents)	38	2003-20	EIGE
	Representation of women in parliaments	190	1997-2018	IPU
	Representation of women in managerial positions	161	2010-19	ILO
	Representation of women in senior and middle management positions	108	2010-19	ILO
	Representation of women on company boards	57	2016-20	MSCI
	Female representation in "manly" jobs and sectors	-	-	-
	Percentage of elected seats held by women in deliberative bodies of local government	115	2018	UN Women
Available indicators				
Legal framework	Number of countries with a legal framework that prohibits women from entering certain professions	180	2009-19	SIGI
	Number of countries with a legal framework that does not allow women to work the same night hours as men	180	2009-19	SIGI
Attitudes	-	-	-	-
Consequences for women's empowerment	-	-	-	-

Table 4.5. Be the "ideal worker"

Indicators tracking progress towards gender-equitable masculine norms

	Indicators	Country coverage	Year	Data source
Ideal indicators				
Legal framework	Number of countries with a legal framework mandating paid paternity leave	180	2009-19	SIGI
	Number of countries with a legal framework mandating parental leave	180	2009-19	SIGI
Attitudes	Percentage of the population agreeing with the following statement: The ideal worker has "masculine attributes"	-	-	-
	Percentage of the population approving of a man taking parental leave to take care of his children	28	2017	Eurobarometer
	Percentage of the population agreeing with the following statement: The ideal worker should prioritise work over family	-	-	-
	Percentage of men reporting that being manly/masculine will help them get a pay rise	4	2019	Ipsos
	Percentage of men reporting that being manly/masculine will help them get or keep a job	4	2019	Ipsos
Consequences for women's empowerment	Female labour force participation and employment rates	141	2010-20	ILO
	Prevalence of female informal employment	38	2010-19	ILO
	Percentage of low-paid workers, among all low-paid workers, who are female	54	2010-19	ILO
	Female labour force participation rate	74	2010-19	ILO
	Number of users of publicly administered paternity leave benefits or publicly administered paid paternity leave per 100 live births	11	2005-16	OECD
Available indicators				
Legal framework	-	-	-	-
Attitudes	-	-	-	-
Consequences for women's empowerment	Percentage of currently working men who took no parental leave after birth of most recent child	15	Various years	IMAGES, Helping Dads Care Research Project

Table 4.6. Be a "manly" leader

Indicators tracking progress towards gender-equitable masculine norms

	Indicators	Country coverage	Year	Data source
Ideal indicators				
Legal framework	Number of countries with a legal framework mandating non-discrimination on the basis of gender in political and economic leadership positions	-	-	-
Attitudes	Percentage of the population agreeing with the following statement: A leader should have patriarchal masculine attributes in order to be successful	-	-	-
	Percentage of the population agreeing with the following statement: In my community, a leader is expected to have patriarchal masculine attributes	-	-	-
Consequences for women's empowerment	Female labour force participation and employment rates	141	2010-20	ILO
	Prevalence of female informal employment	38	2010-19	ILO
	Percentage of low-paid workers, among all low-paid workers, who are female	54	2010-19	ILO
	Female labour force participation rate	74	2010-19	ILO
	Number of users of publicly administered paternity leave benefits or publicly administered paid paternity leave per 100 live births	11	2005-16	OECD
Available indicators				
Legal framework	Number of countries with a legal framework that provides women with the same rights as men to hold public and political office, including in the legislature, executive and judiciary	180	2019	SIGI
Attitudes	Percentage of the population agreeing with the following statement: Men make better political leaders than women do	49	1995/98-2017/20	WVS
	Percentage of the population agreeing with the following statement: Men make better business executives than women do	49	2005/09-2017/20	WVS
	Percentage of women and men agreeing with the following statement: I'd feel uncomfortable if my boss were a woman	27	2019	Ipsos
	Percentage of the population disagreeing with the following statement: I would feel very comfortable having a woman as CEO of a major company in my country	10	2018-20	Reykjavik Index for Leadership
	Percentage of the population disagreeing with the following statement: I would feel very comfortable having a woman as head of government in my country	10	2018-20	Reykjavik Index for Leadership
	Percentage of the population agreeing with the following statement: Women should leave politics to men	5	2017/18	IMAGES
Consequences for women's empowerment	Proportion of elected seats held by women in deliberative bodies of local government	115	2018	UN Women

Table 4.7. Not do unpaid care and domestic work

Indicators tracking progress towards gender-equitable masculine norms

	Indicators	Country coverage	Year	Data source
Ideal indicators				
Legal framework	Number of countries with a legal framework that provides men with the same rights as women to be the legal guardian of their children during marriage, after divorce	180	2019	SIGI
	Number of countries putting in place specific measures to allow fathers to benefit from shared custody after divorce	-	-	-
	Number of countries with a legal framework mandating paid paternity leave.	180	2019	SIGI
	Number of countries with a legal framework mandating parental leave	180	2019	SIGI
Attitudes	Percentage of the population declaring that childcare and housework are not tasks that are suitable for men	-	-	-
	Percentage of the population declaring that: In my community a man who does childcare and housework would be judged	-	-	-
	Percentage of the population associating some household activities with being masculine or feminine, not gender neutral	-	-	-
	Percentage of the population agreeing with the following statement: A man who stays at home to look after his children is less of a man	27	2019	Ipsos
Consequences for women's empowerment	Percentage of the population reporting that they share equally childcare and housework	-	-	-
	The female to male ratio of participation rate in unpaid care and housework, by activity	-	-	-
Available indicators				
Legal framework	-	-	-	-
Attitudes	Percentage of the population disapproving of a man doing an equal share of housework	28	2017	Eurobarometer
	Percentage of respondents agreeing that employers should make it easier for men to combine childcare with work	27	2019	Ipsos
	Percentage of the population finding it acceptable to let women do the majority of housework, childcare and elderly care	17	2021	Focus 2030 and Women Deliver
	Percentage of the population agreeing with the following statement: I think it is shameful when men engage in caring for children or other domestic work	5	2017/19	IMAGES
	Percentage of men agreeing with the following statement: society tells me that a husband shouldn't have to do household chores	3	2017	The Man Box
Consequences for women's empowerment	Female to male ratio of average time spent on unpaid care and domestic work	102	2019	SIGI
	Percentage of ever-married respondents reporting that they participated in cleaning the bathroom, and/or preparing food in the previous month	8	Various years	IMAGES
	Percentage of men reporting that they change diapers of a child (age 0-4 years) several times a week or more	6	Various years	IMAGES
	Percentage of men reporting that they cook for a child (age 0-4 years) several times a week or more	6	Various years	IMAGES

Table 4.8. Have the final say in household decisions

Indicators tracking progress towards gender-equitable masculine norms

	Indicators	Country coverage	Year	Data source
Ideal indicators				
Legal framework	Number of countries with a legal framework providing women with the same rights as men to be recognised as head of household	180	2009-19	SIGI
Attitudes	Percentage of the population agreeing with the following statement: A man should have the final word about decisions in his home [*]	25	Various years	IMAGES
	Percentage of the population agreeing with the following statement: Most people in my community expect men to have the final word about decisions in the home	3	Various years	IMAGES
Consequences for women's empowerment	Percentage of women taking part in the decision-making process at home	-	-	-
Available indicators				
Legal framework	-	-	-	-
Attitudes	Percentage of women and men agreeing with the following statement: A wife does not have the right to challenge her husband's opinions and decisions, even if she disagrees with him	3	Various years	IMAGES
	Percentage of the population agreeing with the following statement: Most people in my community believe that a wife does not have the right to challenge her husband's opinions and decisions even if she disagrees with him	3	Various years	IMAGES
Consequences for women's empowerment	Percentage of women who say that they alone or jointly have the final say in none of the three main decisions (accessing own healthcare; making large purchases; visiting family, relatives, friends)	69	1999-2018	DHS
	Percentage of women who say that they alone or jointly have the final say in none of the three main decisions (accessing own healthcare; making large purchases; visiting family, relatives, friends)	1	2019	IMAGES

Note: This indicator marked with [*] has been collected in 25 countries with slightly different wording. Information on IMAGES data will be completed after Promundo's IMAGES Optimisation process.

Table 4.9. Control household assets

Indicators tracking progress towards gender-equitable masculine norms

	Indicators	Country coverage	Year	Data source
Ideal indicators				
Legal framework	Number of countries with a legal framework that provides women with the same rights as men to administer the household's financial assets	180	2009-19	SIGI
	Number of countries with a legal framework that provides women with the same rights as men to administer the household's land assets	180	2009-19	SIGI
	Number of countries with a legal framework that provides women with the same rights as men to administer the household's non-land and non-financial assets	-	-	-
Attitudes	Percentage of the population declaring that men should have sole decision-making authority over the household's financial assets	-	-	-
	Percentage of the population agreeing that men should have a say in how the money women earn is spent	-	-	-
	Percentage of the population agreeing with the following statement: In my community, men are expected to make the major financial decisions for their households	-	-	-
Consequences for women's empowerment	Percentage of women who report that they take part in the decision-making processes relating to household financial assets on an equal footing with men in the household	-	-	-
	Percentage of women who report that they take part in the decision-making processes relating to non-financial household assets on an equal footing with men in the household	-	-	-
	Percentage of women who report having the final say in how the money they earn is spent	-	-	-
Available indicators				
Legal framework	-	-	-	-
Attitudes	-	-	-	-
Consequences for women's empowerment	Percentage of women for whom the decision-maker regarding major household purchases is mainly the husband	70	1999-2018	DHS
	Percentage of respondents reporting that the husband/man usually makes decisions about large investments [*]	21	Various years	IMAGES
	Percentage of women who report letting their spouse take the lead on long-term financial decisions	10	2019	UBS

Note: Financial assets include formal and informal savings, bank accounts, credit, mortgages, mobile money and other informal financial services. This indicator marked with [*] has been collected in 19 countries with slightly different wording. Information on IMAGES data will be completed after Promundo's IMAGES Optimisation process.

Table 4.10. Protect and exercise guardianship of women in the household

Indicators tracking progress towards gender-equitable masculine norms

	Indicators	Country coverage	Year	Data source
Ideal indicators				
Legal framework	Number of countries with a legal framework that requires a married woman to obey her husband	180	2009-19	SIGI
	Number of countries with a legal framework that includes legal consequences if a wife disobeys her husband	180	2009-19	SIGI
	Number of countries with a legal framework that provides married women with the same rights as married men to choose where to live	180	2009-19	SIGI
	Number of countries with a legal framework that requires women to have permission from their husband/legal guardian to register a business	180	2009-19	SIGI
	Number of countries with a legal framework that requires women to have permission from her husband or legal guardian to work or choose a profession	180	2009-19	SIGI
Attitudes	Percentage of the population agreeing with the following statement: A woman should obey her husband/partner	6	2013	UN multi-country study Asia-Pacific
	Percentage of the population agreeing with the following statement: It is a man's duty to exercise guardianship over female relatives	5	2015-17	IMAGES
	Percentage of the population agreeing with the following statement: In my community, a woman is expected to obey the decisions of her husband/partner	-	-	-
	Percentage of the population agreeing with the following statement: A woman needs to seek approval from her husband/partner before: going outside; working for pay; opening a business; seeking healthcare; visiting friends or family; opening a bank account and/or applying for credit; obtaining a passport; travelling abroad	-	-	-
Consequences for women's empowerment	Percentage of women reporting that they need to seek approval from their husband/partner before: going outside; working for pay; opening a business; seeking healthcare; visiting friends or family; opening a bank account and/or applying for credit; obtaining a passport; travelling abroad	-	-	-
Available indicators				
Legal framework	-	-	-	-
Attitudes	Percentage of the population finding it acceptable for women to always obey her husband	17	2021	Focus 2030 and Women Deliver
	Percentage of women and men agreeing with the following statement: A woman does not have the right to challenge her man's opinions and decisions, even if she disagrees with him	3	Various years	IMAGES
	Percentage of men and women agreeing with the following statement: A married woman should have the same rights to work outside the home as her husband	4	2016	IMAGES
Consequences for women's empowerment	Percentage of ever-married women whose husband/partner insists on knowing where she is at all times	54	2000-18	DHS
	Percentage of women for whom the decision-maker regarding visits to her family or relatives is mainly the husband	69	1999-2018	DHS
	Percentage of women who report that the decision-maker regarding their own healthcare is mainly the husband	70	1999-2018	DHS
	Percentage of women whose husband/partner tries to limit their contact with their family	55	2000-18	DHS

Percentage of ever-married women whose husband/partner does not permit her to meet her female friends	54	2000-18	DHS
Percentage of ever-partnered respondents agreeing with the following statement: Men tell women who she can spend time with [*]	17	Various years	IMAGES
Percentage of ever-partnered respondents agreeing with the following statement: A husband controls when his wife can leave the house [*]	8	Various years	IMAGES

Note: UN multi-country study Asia-Pacific refers to the UN Multi-Country Study on Men and Violence in Asia and the Pacific which has data that cover six urban/rural areas. Data on the indicators marked with [*] have been collected using slightly different wording. Information on IMAGES data will be completed after Promundo's IMAGES Optimisation process.

Table 4.11. Dominates sexual and reproductive choices

Indicators tracking progress towards gender-equitable masculine norms

	Indicators	Country coverage	Year	Data source
Ideal indicators				
Legal framework	Number of countries with a legal framework that requires women to have the approval of the father to seek a legal abortion	180	2009-19	SIGI
	Number of countries where the legal framework's definition of rape covers marital rape	180	2009-19	SIGI
	Number of countries where the domestic violence legislation covers sexual abuse	180	2009-19	SIGI
Attitudes	Percentage of the population believing that a woman is not justified in proposing condom use	-	-	-
	Percentage of the population disagreeing that men and women should decide together whether they want to have children, when and how many	-	-	-
	Percentage of the population agreeing with the following statement: If a husband/partner provides financially, his wife is obliged to have sex with him whenever he wants	4	2015-17	IMAGES
	Percentage of the population agreeing with the following statement: In my community, most people believe that if a husband/partner provides financially, his wife is obliged to have sex with him whenever he wants	-	-	-
	Percentage of women and men agreeing with the following statement: I think a woman cannot refuse to have sex with her husband	6	2013	UN multi-country study Asia-Pacific
Consequences for women's empowerment	Percentage of women declaring not using contraception or accessing family planning because of their husband's/partner's refusal	2	2020	SIGI Country Studies
	Percentage of women declaring having refused sexual intercourse with their husband/partner without facing adverse consequences	-	-	-
	Percentage of women reporting that they took the decision about whether and how many children to have together with their husband/partner	-	-	-
Available indicators				
Legal framework	-	-	-	-
Attitudes	Percentage of women and men reporting that a woman is justified in refusing to have sexual intercourse with her husband if: she knows he has sex with other women; he has a sexually transmitted disease; she has recently given birth; she is tired or not in the mood	65, 50, 36, 78	Various years	DHS
	Percentage of women and men reporting that a wife is justified in asking that her husband use a condom if she knows that he has a sexually transmitted disease	60	2003-18	DHS
	Percentage of the population finding it unacceptable for a woman to refuse sexual intercourse with her partner	17	2021	Focus 2030 and Women Deliver
	Percentage of men agreeing with the following statement: If a husband provides financially, his wife is obliged to have sex with him whenever he wants	4	2015-17	IMAGES
	Percentage of women and men who agree that a husband is justified in hitting or beating his wife if she refuses to have sex with him	70	1999-2018	DHS
	Percentage of men reporting that they would be outraged if their wife asked them to use a condom	5	2011	IMAGES

| Consequences for women's empowerment | Percentage of respondents reporting that the husband has the final say on the use of contraception [*] | 11 | Various years | IMAGES |
| | Percentage of women with an unmet need for family planning | 78 | 1990-2018 | DHS |

Note UN multi-country study Asia-Pacific refers to the UN Multi-Country Study on Men and Violence in Asia and the Pacific which has data that cover six urban/rural areas. Data on this indicator marked with [*] have been collected in ten countries, using slightly different wording. Information on IMAGES data will be completed after Promundo's IMAGES Optimisation process.

Conclusion

By identifying ten norms of restrictive masculinities and outlining indicators to measure them, this publication aims to pinpoint new avenues to promote women's empowerment. Indeed, promoting women's empowerment requires that restrictive masculinities be systematically addressed and measured as hidden drivers of gender inequality. As a starting point on the path to measurement, Chapter 2 and Chapter 3 identified and described ten norms of restrictive masculinities. With these ten norms identified, Chapter 4 has outlined lists of indicators that can be used to measure these norms by accounting for legal frameworks, attitudes and the associated practices that lead to serious consequences for women's empowerment. By including these three types of indicators, efforts to measure these norms can reveal how widely accepted restrictive masculinities are within a population as a starting point for efforts to transform these restrictive masculinities into gender-equitable alternatives.

Measuring masculine norms can support evidence-based policy making for transformation. The ability to measure masculine norms can aid evidence-based policy making by identifying the most important norms to be urgently addressed and, over time, to measure progress in changing these norms into more gender-equitable masculinities. Measuring how masculine norms change over time can provide evidence regarding the effectiveness of policies and interventions aimed at transforming restrictive masculinities into gender-equitable ones. With the data for each of the ideal indicators listed in the tables in this chapter, it would be possible to construct a conceptual framework to measure the current status of masculine norms at the national, regional and international levels. This framework can guide efforts to systematically analyse masculine norms which, in turn, can accelerate gender equality by identifying which norms are barriers to change and demonstrating the ways that gender equality benefits all people.

Annex A. Data sources and country/territory coverage

Table A.1. Countries/territories covered by the indicators presented in this publication

Data source	List of countries/territories covered
Demographic and Health Surveys (DHS) (n.d.)	Afghanistan, Albania, Angola, Armenia, Azerbaijan, Bangladesh, Benin, Plurinational State of Bolivia, Brazil, Burkina Faso, Burundi, Cambodia, Cameroon, Central African Republic, Chad, Colombia, Comoros, Republic of the Congo, Côte d'Ivoire, Democratic Republic of the Congo, Dominican Republic, Egypt, Eritrea, Eswatini, Ethiopia, Gabon, Gambia, Ghana, Guatemala, Guinea, Guyana, Haiti, Honduras, India, Indonesia, Jordan, Kazakhstan, Kenya, Kyrgyzstan, Lesotho, Liberia, Madagascar, Malawi, Maldives, Mali, Mauritania, Republic of Moldova, Morocco, Mozambique, Myanmar, Namibia, Nepal, Nicaragua, Niger, Nigeria, Pakistan, Papua New Guinea, Paraguay, Peru, Philippines, Rwanda, Sao Tome and Principe, Senegal, Sierra Leone, South Africa, Tajikistan, Timor-Leste, Togo, Turkey, Turkmenistan, Uganda, Ukraine, United Republic of Tanzania, Uzbekistan, Viet Nam, Yemen, Zambia, and Zimbabwe
European Institute for Gender Equality (EIGE) (2020)	Albania, Austria, Belgium, Bosnia and Herzegovina, Bulgaria, Croatia, Cyprus, Czech Republic, Denmark, Estonia, Finland, France, Germany, Greece, Hungary, Iceland, Ireland, Italy, Kosovo, Latvia, Liechtenstein, Lithuania, Luxembourg, Malta, Montenegro, Netherlands, Norway, Poland, Portugal, Republic of North Macedonia, Romania, Serbia, Slovak Republic, Slovenia, Spain, Sweden, Turkey, and United Kingdom
Eurobarometer (2017)	Austria, Belgium, Bulgaria, Croatia, Cyprus, Czech Republic, Denmark, Estonia, Finland, France, Germany, Greece, Hungary, Ireland, Italy, Latvia, Lithuania, Luxembourg, Malta, Netherlands, Poland, Portugal, Romania, Slovak Republic, Slovenia, Spain, Sweden, and United Kingdom
Focus 2030 and Women Deliver (2021)	Argentina, Australia, Canada, People's Republic of China, Colombia, France, Germany, India, Japan, Kenya, Mexico, New Zealand, South Africa, Switzerland, Tunisia, United Kingdom and United States
Helping Dads Care Research Project (2017-19)	Argentina, Brazil, Canada, Japan, Netherlands, United Kingdom and United States
ILOStat (various)	Afghanistan, Albania, Algeria, Angola, Antigua and Barbuda, Argentina, Armenia, Australia, Austria, Azerbaijan, Bahamas, Bahrain, Bangladesh, Barbados, Belarus, Belgium, Belize, Bhutan, Plurinational State of Bolivia, Bosnia and Herzegovina, Botswana, Brazil, Brunei Darussalam, Bulgaria, Burkina Faso, Burundi, Cabo Verde, Cambodia, Cameroon, Canada, Chile, Comoros, Cook Islands, Costa Rica, Côte d'Ivoire, Croatia, Cuba, Curaçao, Cyprus, Czech Republic, Democratic Republic of the Congo, Denmark, Dominica, Dominican Republic, Ecuador, Egypt, El Salvador, Estonia, Eswatini, Ethiopia, Fiji, Finland, France, Gambia, Georgia, Germany, Ghana, Greece, Guatemala, Guyana, Haiti, Honduras, Hungary, Iceland, India, Indonesia, Islamic Republic of Iran, Iraq, Ireland, Israel, Italy, Jamaica, Japan, Jordan, Kazakhstan, Kenya, Kiribati, Korea, Kosovo, Kuwait, Kyrgyzstan, Lao People's Democratic Republic, Latvia, Lebanon, Lesotho, Liberia, Lithuania, Luxembourg, Madagascar, Malawi, Malaysia, Maldives, Mali, Malta, Mauritius, Mexico, Federated States of Micronesia, Republic of Moldova, Mongolia, Montenegro, Morocco, Mozambique, Myanmar, Namibia, Nauru, Nepal, Netherlands, New Zealand, Nicaragua, Niger, Nigeria, Norway, Oman, Pakistan, Palau, Palestinian Authority, Panama, Papua New Guinea, Paraguay, Peru, Philippines, Poland, Portugal, Qatar, Republic of North Macedonia, Romania, Russian Federation, Rwanda, Saint Lucia, Saint Vincent and the Grenadines, Samoa, Sao Tome and Principe, Saudi Arabia, Senegal, Serbia, Seychelles, Sierra Leone, Singapore, Slovak Republic, Slovenia, Solomon Islands, South Africa, Spain, Sri Lanka, Suriname, Sweden, Switzerland, Syrian Arab Republic, Tajikistan, United Republic of Tanzania, Thailand, Timor-Leste, Togo, Tonga, Trinidad and Tobago, Tunisia, Turkey, Tuvalu, Uganda, Ukraine, United Arab Emirates, United Kingdom, United States, Uruguay, Vanuatu,

	Bolivarian Republic of Venezuela, Viet Nam, Yemen, Zambia, and Zimbabwe
IPU Parline (various)	Afghanistan, Albania, Algeria, Andorra, Angola, Antigua and Barbuda, Argentina, Armenia, Australia, Austria, Barbados, Belarus, Belgium, Belize, Benin, Bhutan, Plurinational State of Bolivia, Bosnia and Herzegovina, Botswana, Brazil, Brunei Darussalam, Bulgaria, Burkina Faso, Burundi, Cabo Verde, Cambodia, Cameroon, Canada, Colombia, Comoros, Republic of the Congo, Costa Rica, Côte d'Ivoire, Croatia, Cuba, Cyprus, Czech Republic, Democratic People's Republic of Korea, Democratic Republic of the Congo, Denmark, Djibouti, Dominica, Dominican Republic, Ecuador, Egypt, El Salvador, Equatorial Guinea, Eritrea, Estonia, Eswatini, Ethiopia, Fiji, Finland, France, Gabon, Gambia, Georgia, Germany, Ghana, Greece, Grenada, Guatemala, Guinea, Guinea-Bissau, Guyana, Haiti, Honduras, Hungary, Iceland, India, Indonesia, Islamic Republic of Iran, Iraq, Ireland, Israel, Italy, Jamaica, Japan, Jordan, Kazakhstan, Kenya, Kiribati, Korea, Kuwait, Kyrgyzstan, Lao People's Democratic Republic, Latvia, Lebanon, Lesotho, Liberia, Libya, Liechtenstein, Lithuania, Luxembourg, Madagascar, Malawi, Malaysia, Maldives, Mali, Malta, Marshall Islands, Mauritania, Mauritius, Mexico, Federated States of Micronesia, Republic of Moldova, Monaco, Mongolia, Montenegro, Morocco, Mozambique, Myanmar, Namibia, Nauru, Nepal, Netherlands, New Zealand, Nicaragua, Niger, Nigeria, Norway, Oman, Pakistan, Palau, Panama, Papua New Guinea, Paraguay, Peru, Philippines, Poland, Portugal, Qatar, Republic of North Macedonia, Romania, Russian Federation, Rwanda, Saint Kitts and Nevis, Saint Lucia, Saint Vincent and the Grenadines, Samoa, San Marino, Sao Tome and Principe, Saudi Arabia, Senegal, Serbia, Seychelles, Sierra Leone, Singapore, Slovak Republic, Slovenia, Solomon Islands, Somalia, South Africa, South Sudan, Spain, Sri Lanka, Sudan, Suriname, Sweden, Switzerland, Syrian Arab Republic, Tajikistan, United Republic of Tanzania, Thailand, Timor-Leste, Togo, Tonga, Trinidad and Tobago, Tunisia, Turkey, Turkmenistan, Tuvalu, Uganda, Ukraine, United Arab Emirates, United Kingdom, United States, Uruguay, Uzbekistan, Vanuatu, Bolivarian Republic of Venezuela, Viet Nam, Yemen, Zambia, and Zimbabwe
Ipsos (2019a)	Argentina, Australia, Belgium, Brazil, Canada, Chile, Colombia, France, Germany, Hungary, India, Italy, Japan, Korea, Malaysia, Mexico, Netherlands, Peru, Poland, Russian Federation, Serbia, South Africa, Spain, Sweden, Turkey, United Kingdom, and United States
Ipsos (2019b)	Australia, Canada, United Kingdom, and United States
International Men and Gender Equality Survey (IMAGES) (various)	Afghanistan, Azerbaijan, Bosnia and Herzegovina, Brazil, Chile, Croatia, Democratic Republic of the Congo, Egypt, Georgia, India, Kosovo, Kuwait, Lebanon, Mali, Mexico, Republic of Moldova, Morocco, Mozambique, Nicaragua, Niger, Nigeria, Pakistan, Palestinian Authority, Rwanda, Serbia, United Republic of Tanzania, Uganda, Ukraine, and Viet Nam.
The Man Box study (2017)	Mexico, United Kingdom and United States
MSCI (2016-20)	Argentina; Australia; Austria; Belgium; Bermuda; Brazil; Canada; Cayman Islands; Chile; People's Republic of China; Colombia; Cyprus; Czech Republic; Denmark; Egypt; Finland; France; Germany; Greece; Hong Kong, China; Hungary; India; Indonesia; Ireland; Isle of Man; Japan; Bailiwick of Jersey; Korea; Luxembourg; Macau, China; Malaysia; Mexico; Netherlands; New Zealand; Norway; Pakistan; Papua New Guinea; Peru; Philippines; Poland; Portugal; Qatar; Russian Federation; Saudi Arabia; Singapore; South Africa; Spain; Sweden; Switzerland; Chinese Taipei; Thailand; Turkey; United Arab Emirates; United Kingdom; and United States
Programme for International Student Assessment (PISA) (2018)	Albania; Argentina; Australia; Austria; Azerbaijan (Baku City only); Belarus; Belgium; Bosnia and Herzegovina; Brazil; Brunei Darussalam; Bulgaria; Canada; Chile; People's Republic of China; Colombia; Costa Rica; Croatia; Czech Republic; Denmark; Dominican Republic; Estonia; Finland; France; Georgia; Germany; Greece; Hong Kong, China; Hungary; Iceland; Indonesia; Ireland; Israel; Italy; Japan; Jordan; Kazakhstan; Korea; Kosovo; Latvia; Lebanon; Lithuania; Luxembourg; Macau, China; Malaysia; Malta; Mexico; Republic of Moldova; Montenegro; Morocco; Netherlands; New Zealand; Norway; Panama; Peru; Philippines; Poland; Portugal; Qatar; Republic of North Macedonia; Romania; Russian Federation; Saudi Arabia; Serbia; Singapore; Slovak Republic; Slovenia; Spain; Sweden; Switzerland; Chinese Taipei; Thailand; Turkey; Ukraine; United Arab Emirates; United Kingdom (excluding Scotland); United Kingdom (Scotland); United States; Uruguay; and Viet Nam
Reykjavik Index for Leadership (2019-20/21)	Brazil, Canada, People's Republic of China, France, Germany, India, Italy, Japan, Kenya, Nigeria, Russian Federation, United Kingdom, and United States
Social Institutions and Gender Index (SIGI) (2019)	Afghanistan; Albania; Algeria; Angola; Antigua and Barbuda; Argentina; Armenia; Australia; Austria; Azerbaijan; Bahamas; Bahrain; Bangladesh; Barbados; Belarus; Belgium; Belize; Benin; Bhutan; Plurinational State of Bolivia; Bosnia and Herzegovina; Botswana; Brazil; Brunei Darussalam; Bulgaria; Burkina Faso; Burundi; Cabo Verde; Cambodia; Cameroon; Canada; Central African Republic; Chad; Chile; People's Republic of China; Colombia;

	Republic of the Congo; Comoros; Costa Rica; Côte d'Ivoire; Croatia; Cuba; Cyprus; Czech Republic; Democratic Republic of the Congo; Denmark; Djibouti; Dominica; Dominican Republic; Ecuador; Egypt; El Salvador; Equatorial Guinea; Eritrea; Estonia; Eswatini; Ethiopia; Fiji; Finland; France; Gabon; Gambia; Georgia; Germany; Ghana; Greece; Grenada; Guatemala; Guinea; Guinea-Bissau; Guyana; Haiti; Honduras; Hong Kong, China; Hungary; Iceland; India; Indonesia; Islamic Republic of Iran; Iraq; Ireland; Israel; Italy; Jamaica; Japan; Jordan; Kazakhstan; Kenya; Korea; Kosovo; Kuwait; Kyrgyzstan; Lao People's Democratic Republic; Latvia; Lebanon; Lesotho; Liberia; Libya; Lithuania; Luxembourg; Madagascar; Malawi; Malaysia; Maldives; Mali; Malta; Mauritania; Mauritius; Mexico; Republic of Moldova; Mongolia; Montenegro; Morocco; Mozambique; Myanmar; Namibia; Nepal; Netherlands; New Zealand; Nicaragua; Niger; Nigeria; Norway; Oman; Pakistan; Palestinian Authority; Panama; Papua New Guinea; Paraguay; Peru; Philippines; Poland; Portugal; Qatar; Republic of North Macedonia; Romania; Russian Federation; Rwanda; Samoa; Sao Tome and Principe; Saudi Arabia; Senegal; Serbia; Seychelles; Sierra Leone; Singapore; Slovak Republic; Slovenia; Solomon Islands; Somalia; South Africa; South Sudan; Spain; Sri Lanka; Sudan; Sweden; Switzerland; Syrian Arab Republic; Chinese Taipei; Tajikistan; United Republic of Tanzania; Thailand; Timor-Leste; Togo; Trinidad and Tobago; Tunisia; Turkey; Turkmenistan; Uganda; Ukraine; United Arab Emirates; United Kingdom; United States; Uruguay; Uzbekistan; Bolivarian Republic of Venezuela; Viet Nam; Yemen; Zambia; and Zimbabwe
SIGI country studies (various)	Burkina Faso, United Republic of Tanzania (forthcoming), Uganda
Union Bank of Switzerland (UBS) (2020)	Brazil; Germany; Hong Kong, China; Italy; Mexico; Singapore; Switzerland; United Kingdom; and United States
UN Multi-Country Study on Men and Violence in Asia and the Pacific (2013)	Bangladesh (urban site: Dhaka, rural site: Matlab), Cambodia (national), People's Republic of China (one country in the central region with urban and rural areas), Indonesia (urban site: Jakarta, rural site: Purworejo, Papua site: Jayapura), Papua New Guinea (site: Bougainville), and Sri Lanka (national)
UN Women (2018)	Afghanistan; Albania; Algeria; American Samoa; Andorra; Antigua and Barbuda; Armenia; Australia; Austria; Azerbaijan; Bahrain; Bangladesh; Barbados; Belarus; Belgium; Belize; Benin; Bhutan; Plurinational State of Bolivia; Bosnia and Herzegovina; Botswana; Brazil; Brunei Darussalam; Bulgaria; Burkina Faso; Burundi; Cabo Verde; Cambodia; Cameroon; Canada; Chile; People's Republic of China; Colombia; Comoros; Costa Rica; Côte d'Ivoire; Croatia; Cuba; Czech Republic; Denmark; Djibouti; Dominican Republic; Ecuador; Egypt; El Salvador; Equatorial Guinea; Estonia; Eswatini; Finland; France; Georgia; Germany; Ghana; Grenada; Guam; Guatemala; Guinea; Honduras; Hungary; Iceland; India; Indonesia; Islamic Republic of Iran; Iraq; Ireland; Israel; Italy; Jamaica; Japan; Jordan; Kazakhstan; Kenya; Korea; Kuwait; Lao People's Democratic Republic; Latvia; Lebanon; Lesotho; Liberia; Liechtenstein; Lithuania; Luxembourg; Macau, China; Malawi; Maldives; Mali; Malta; Marshall Islands; Mauritania; Mauritius; Mexico; Republic of Moldova; Mongolia; Montenegro; Morocco; Myanmar; Namibia; Nepal; Netherlands; New Caledonia; New Zealand; Niger; Nigeria; Northern Mariana Islands; Norway; Oman; Pakistan; Palestinian Authority; Panama; Paraguay; Peru; Philippines; Poland; Qatar; Romania; Rwanda; Saint Kitts and Nevis; Saint Lucia; Saint Vincent and the Grenadines; Samoa; San Marino; Saudi Arabia; Senegal; Serbia; Seychelles; Sierra Leone; Singapore; Slovak Republic; Slovenia; Somalia; South Africa; Spain; Sri Lanka; Sudan; Suriname; Sweden; Switzerland; Syrian Arab Republic; United Republic of Tanzania, Thailand; Timor-Leste; Togo; Tonga; Tunisia; Turkey; Tuvalu; Uganda; United Arab Emirates; United Kingdom; Uruguay; Vanuatu; Viet Nam; Yemen; Zambia; and Zimbabwe
World Health Organization (WHO) Multi-country Study on Women's Health and Domestic Violence against Women (2005)	Bangladesh (urban site: Dhaka, rural site: Matlab), Brazil (urban site: São Paulo, rural site: Zona da Mata de Pernambuco), Ethiopia (rural site: Butajira), Japan (urban site: Yokohama), Namibia (urban site: Windhoek), Peru (urban site: Lima, rural site: Department of Cusco), Samoa (national), Serbia and Montenegro (urban site: Belgrade), United Republic of Tanzania (urban site: Dar es Salaam, rural site: Mbeya district), and Thailand (urban site: Bangkok, rural site: Nakhonsawan)
Women, Business and the Law (WBL) (2020)	Afghanistan; Albania; Algeria; Angola; Antigua and Barbuda; Argentina; Armenia; Australia; Austria; Azerbaijan; Bahamas; Bahrain; Bangladesh; Barbados; Belarus; Belgium; Belize; Benin; Bhutan; Plurinational State of Bolivia; Bosnia and Herzegovina; Botswana; Brazil; Brunei Darussalam; Bulgaria; Burkina Faso; Burundi; Cabo Verde; Cambodia; Cameroon; Canada; Central African Republic; Chad; Chile; People's Republic of China; Colombia; Comoros; Republic of the Congo; Costa Rica; Côte d'Ivoire; Croatia; Cyprus; Czech Republic; Democratic Republic of the Congo; Denmark; Djibouti; Dominica; Dominican Republic; Ecuador; Egypt; El Salvador; Equatorial Guinea; Eritrea; Estonia; Eswatini; Ethiopia; Fiji; Finland; France; Gabon; Gambia; Georgia; Germany; Ghana; Greece; Grenada; Guatemala; Guinea;

	Guinea-Bissau; Guyana; Haiti; Honduras; Hong Kong, China; Hungary; Iceland; India; Indonesia; Islamic Republic of Iran; Iraq; Ireland; Israel; Italy; Jamaica; Japan; Jordan; Kazakhstan; Kenya; Kiribati; Korea; Kosovo; Kuwait; Kyrgyzstan; Lao People's Democratic Republic; Latvia; Lebanon; Lesotho; Liberia; Libya; Lithuania; Luxembourg; Madagascar; Malawi; Malaysia; Maldives; Mali; Malta; Marshall Islands; Mauritania; Mauritius; Mexico; Federated States of Micronesia; Republic of Moldova; Mongolia; Montenegro; Morocco; Mozambique; Myanmar; Namibia; Nepal; Netherlands; New Zealand; Nicaragua; Niger; Nigeria; Norway; Oman; Pakistan; Palau; Palestinian Authority; Panama; Papua New Guinea; Paraguay; Peru; Philippines; Poland; Portugal; Puerto Rico; Qatar; Republic of North Macedonia; Romania; Russian Federation; Rwanda; Saint Kitts and Nevis; Saint Lucia; Saint Vincent and the Grenadines; Samoa; San Marino; Sao Tome and Principe; Saudi Arabia; Senegal; Serbia; Seychelles; Sierra Leone; Singapore; Slovak Republic; Slovenia; Solomon Islands; Somalia; South Africa; South Sudan; Spain; Sri Lanka; Sudan; Suriname; Sweden; Switzerland; Syrian Arab Republic; Chinese Taipei; United Republic of Tanzania; Tajikistan; Thailand; Timor-Leste; Togo; Tonga; Trinidad and Tobago; Tunisia; Turkey; Uganda; Ukraine; United Arab Emirates; United Kingdom; United States; Uruguay; Uzbekistan; Vanuatu; Bolivarian Republic of Venezuela; Viet Nam; Yemen; Zambia; and Zimbabwe
World Values Survey (WVS-7) (2017-20)	Argentina; Australia; Bangladesh; Plurinational State of Bolivia; Brazil; Chile; People's Republic of China; Colombia; Cyprus; Ecuador; Egypt; Ethiopia; Germany; Greece; Guatemala; Hong Kong, China; Indonesia; Islamic Republic of Iran; Iraq; Japan; Jordan; Kazakhstan; Korea; Kyrgyzstan; Lebanon; Macau, China; Malaysia; Mexico; Myanmar; New Zealand; Nicaragua; Nigeria; Pakistan; Peru; Philippines; Puerto Rico; Romania; Russian Federation; Serbia; Chinese Taipei; Tajikistan; Thailand; Tunisia; Turkey; United States; Viet Nam; and Zimbabwe
WVS Gender Module (2020)	Ethiopia and Zimbabwe

www.ingramcontent.com/pod-product-compliance
Lightning Source LLC
Chambersburg PA
CBHW082110210326
41599CB00033B/6652